An Oracle of Ancient Egypt

An Oracle of Ancient Egypt

The Eye of Horus

DAVID LAWSON

This book is dedicated to two special friends.
To Susan Mears, thank you for breathing life into *The Eye of Horus* and for giving me the opportunity to write. To the memory of Francesca Montaldi, your love and vision will live on in the hearts of the many people whose lives you touched.
With love, David

First published in Great Britain in 1996 by Piatkus Books under the title *The Eye of Horus*.

A Connections Book
This edition published in Great Britain in 1998 by
Connections Book Publishing Limited
St Chad's House
148 King's Cross Road
London WC1X 9DH

1 3 5 7 9 10 8 6 4 2

British Library Cataloguing-in-Publication data available on request

ISBN 1 85906 011 0

AN EDDISON•SADD EDITION
Edited, designed and produced by
Eddison Sadd Editions Limited
St Chad's House, 148 King's Cross Road
London WC1X 9DH

Phototypeset in Bodoni BT and Calligraphic 421 BT using QuarkXPress on Apple Macintosh.
Origination by SX Composing, Raleigh, Essex
Printed and assembled in China by Leo Paper Products.
Stones and bag manufactured in China by The Shanghai Connection

CONTENTS

INTRODUCTION

Thank you for choosing *The Eye of Horus*. I trust that this book will provide you with guidance, inspiration and insights for years to come. The Eye of Horus is an ancient-Egyptian symbol of protection, intuition, healing and personal vision. For Egyptians, it had connections with the heavenly realms and was used as a kind of 'evil eye', to ward off danger, illness and bad fortune. Its likeness turns up again and again within the symbology of many spiritual traditions around the world.

Many of us are fascinated with the culture, architecture, myths and legends of the ancient Egyptians. Even those who have never visited the modern state of Egypt, to stand beside the pyramids or to travel down the Nile in a felucca, feel a strange connection to the legendary past of this country.

Perhaps we are drawn to the magnificence of the monuments the Egyptians left behind, or perhaps we are curious about the early stirrings of civilization that we can learn about from ancient hieroglyphs. The achievements of the Egyptians are indicative of an extraordinary leap of consciousness that humankind has passed through, and this period of history may even give us clues to the greater process of human evolution. Many people believe that they were actually there, living out, not just one, but many former lives in their cycle of reincarnation. Others believe that they are linked to the ancient Egyptians through a collective memory that we can all draw from. Whatever the truth is for each of us, the symbology, beliefs and culture of these fascinating people have much to teach us about ourselves and the lives that we are leading today.

The Legacy of the Egyptians

It is perhaps the funerary practices of the ancient Egyptians that have given us most of the information we have about their world. Their fascination with life after death has provided us with treasures, artifacts and detailed accounts of lives, legends and beliefs. Pictures and hieroglyphic inscriptions on the walls of tombs and temples tell us about their elaborate rituals, their conquests and their political and religious changes. The knowledge that we have of them is really based on the lives and aspirations of royalty and their noble aides. We know much less about the lives of ordinary people because common housing and burial structures were not built to withstand the sands of time. However, we do have a wealth of information about the gods, goddesses and spiritual practices that were an integral part of the collective belief system of this first, great nation state.

The Gods and Goddesses of the Egyptians

The gods and goddesses of the ancient Egyptians are representative of human concerns as well as spiritual ones. They give us insights into the minds of the Egyptians, their hopes and fears, their beliefs in the greater order of the universe and their governmental administration. Like all people, the Egyptians were fascinated with their origins and they had a need to explain the world around them. Some gods are the central figures in creation myths and they have similarities to the universal god of Judaeo-Christian belief, the origins of which were geographically close to ancient Egypt. Other gods were elemental in nature and were indicative of the need to explain the earth, the sky, the sun and the many other mysterious forces of the universe. As the Egyptians developed their civilization and formalized their government, their gods and goddesses reflected this and deities became associated with the subjects of sovereignty, administration and architecture.

Some theories about the origins of the Egyptians and their gods postulate that the gods were really advanced beings from a highly civilized culture that preceded the civilized world as we know it. These highly evolved people are thought to have sown the seeds of civilization throughout the ancient world, particularly in the Middle East, North Africa and Central America. The existence of such peoples would certainly help to explain the mysterious technologies that were used in the construction of the pyramids. According to some sources, these super-beings are imagined to have come from a sophisticated culture that existed before major planetary changes wiped out most of the Earth's population. Other theorists imagine them to be visitors from another solar system who stimulated our development before moving on to other worlds. Whatever we believe, the gods and goddesses of the Egyptians are powerful human and spiritual archetypes.

In the modern world, we have developed many more sophisticated structures of civilization and complex technologies than the Egyptians. We have also developed sciences that are able to explain a great deal about the world we live in. In spite of this, many of the basic questions that intrigued the ancient Egyptians still remain unanswered. What are our spiritual origins? What is the purpose of our lives? What will happen to us after we die? The gods and goddesses of the Egyptians are a valuable resource that can help us to look inside ourselves and to make sense of our existence.

The Cult Centres

Prior to the creation of a nation state, Egypt was a collection of self-governing regions, or *nomes*, each with its own cults, spiritual practices and beliefs. As Egypt developed, certain cult centres grew in strength and influence, and the worship of regional gods spread to other areas *(see map on page 8)*. It is the powerful cults that have provided us with the most information about the Egyptian pantheon, as well as a number of Greek sources that drew comparisons between the Egyptian gods and their own deities. The cult centre of Heliopolis or Yunu had a powerful hierarchy of gods that spanned the myths of creation, the wonders of the natural world and the concerns of

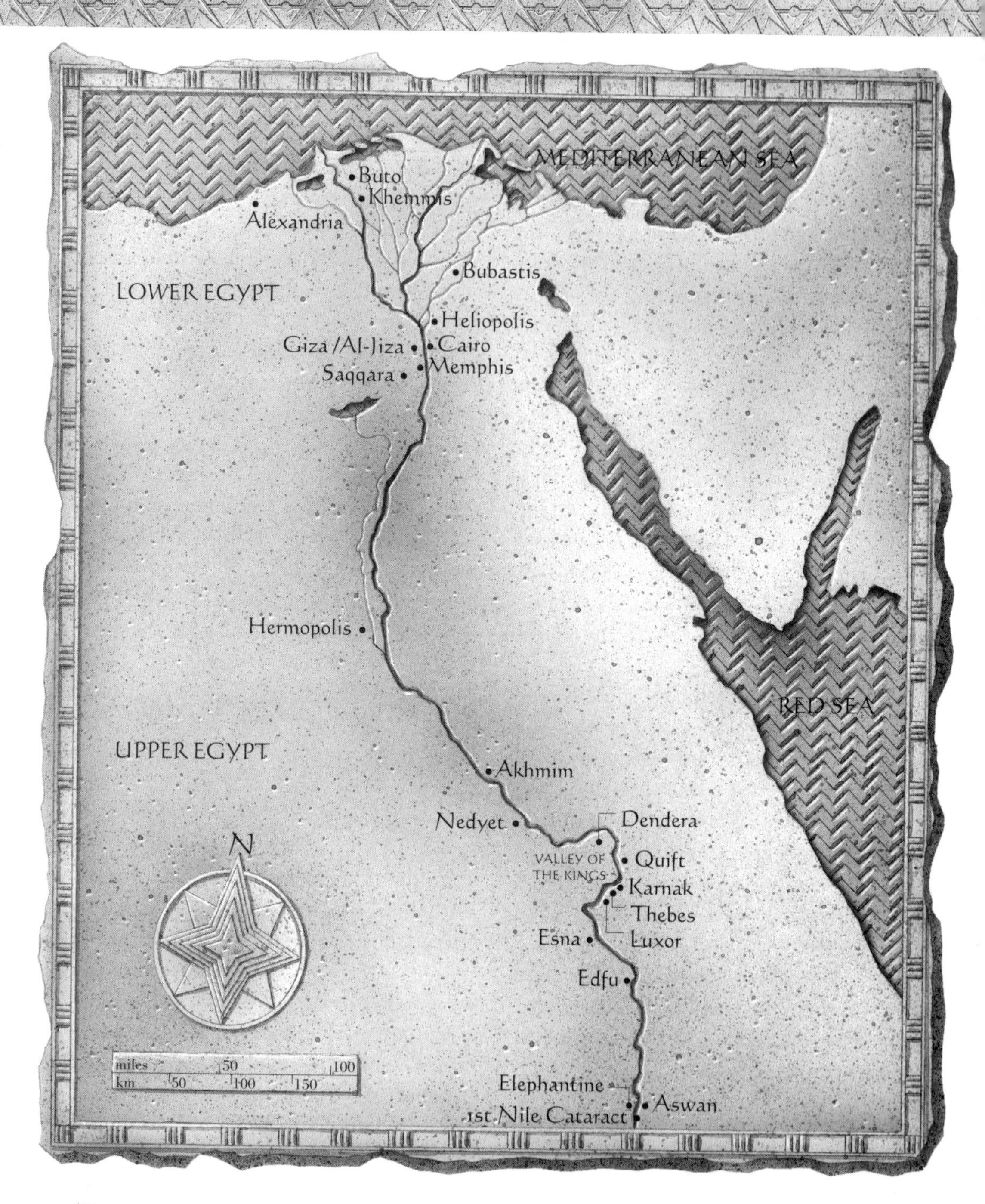

Upper and Lower Egypt showing major cult centres and sites mentioned in the text.

government. Other major cult centres existed at Memphis, Hermopolis and Thebes, and it is chiefly the myths and legends of these four ancient sites that provide us with the background information for the stone tablets described in this book.

The Relationships of the Gods and Goddesses

Many of the Egyptian gods and goddesses were thought to be related to each other and some were imagined to have definite lineage. Placing gods into family groups was a way of rationalizing their position and importance. As the popularity of a regional god grew to a level of national influence, they were often incorporated into the family group or hierarchy at other cult centres. Many areas favoured triads, consisting of a divine patriarch, a divine matriarch and a divine child. Other centres had more complex groupings of deities. The 'family trees' overleaf show some of the gods and goddesses that are featured within this book, placed in their sacred relationships.

The Dynasties of Egypt

The information concerning each god and goddess featured within *The Eye of Horus* is not only rationalized from the mythological variations associated with different sites, but it also reflects chronological variations that occur throughout a period of approximately three thousand years of Egyptian history. Below is a brief chronology to help you place any references to specific periods or dynasties into context. While it reflects current and established opinion of chronological order, it is perhaps wise to state that there are other opinions that differ from the mainstream, and new evidence may yet alter our view of this.

PERIOD	DATES	DYNASTY
Predynastic	up to 3050 BC	———
Early Dynastic	3050 – 2686 BC	Dynasties I – II
Old Kingdom	2686 – 2181 BC	Dynasties III – VI
First Intermediate Period	2181 – 2040 BC	Dynasties VII – XI
Middle Kingdom	2040 – 1782 BC	Dynasties XI – XII
Second Intermediate Period	1782 – 1570 BC	Dynasties XIII – XVII
New Kingdom	1570 – 1070 BC	Dynasties XVIII – XX
Third Intermediate Period	1070 – 664 BC	Dynasties XXI – XXV
Late Period	664 – 332 BC	Dynasties XXVI – XXXI
Greco-Roman Period	332 BC – AD 395	———

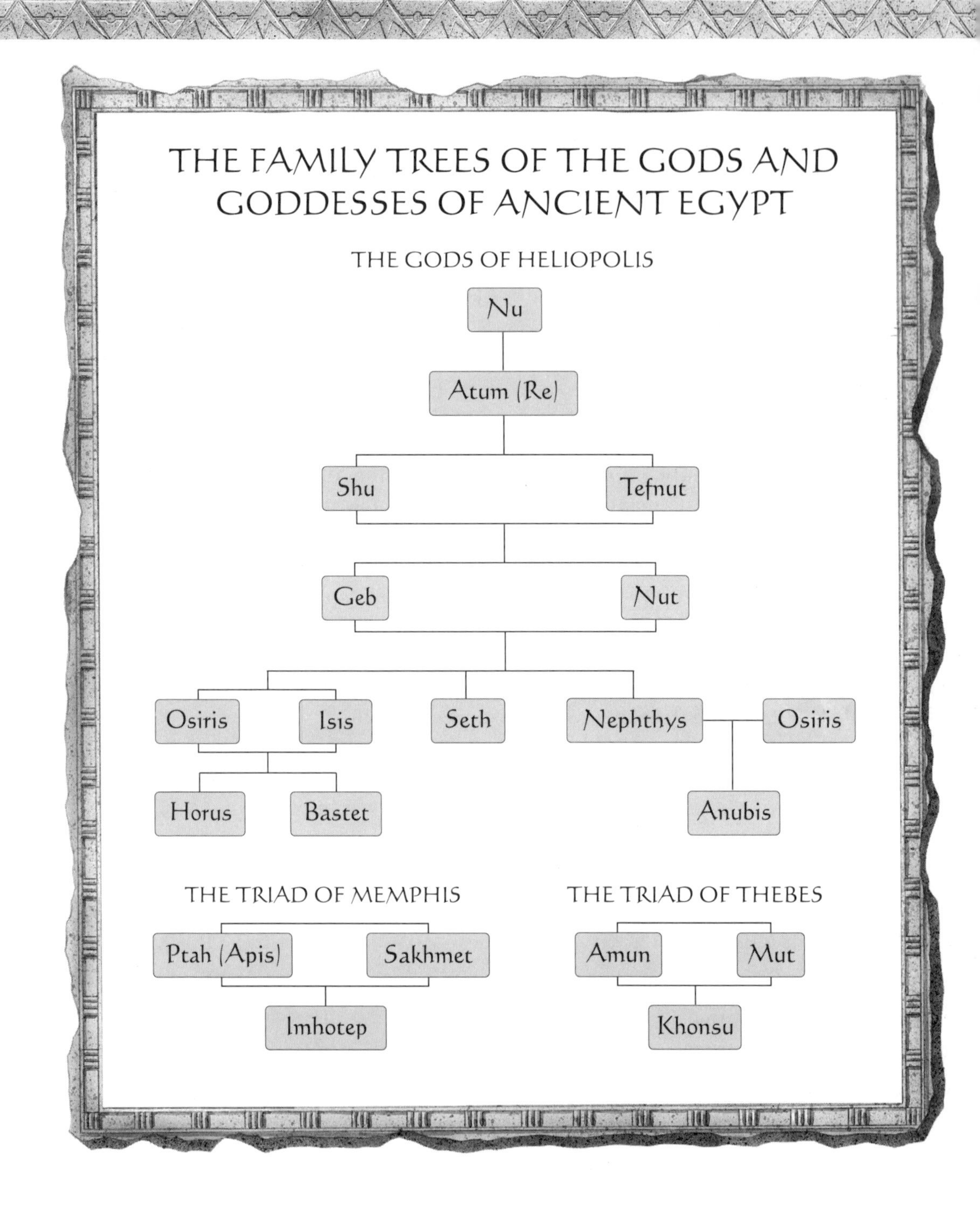
THE FAMILY TREES OF THE GODS AND GODDESSES OF ANCIENT EGYPT
THE GODS OF HELIOPOLIS
Nu
Atum (Re)
Shu
Tefnut
Geb
Nut
Osiris
Isis
Seth
Nephthys
Osiris
Horus
Bastet
Anubis
THE TRIAD OF MEMPHIS
Ptah (Apis)
Sakhmet
Imhotep
THE TRIAD OF THEBES
Amun
Mut
Khonsu

PART ONE

GETTING STARTED

'I am Horus who came forth from the Eye of Horus, I am Wadjet who came forth from Horus, I am Horus who flew up ...'

THE ANCIENT EGYPTIAN BOOK OF THE DEAD

'Cometh Horus upon the waters of his father ...'

THE EGYPTIAN BOOK OF THE DEAD

When we combine our personal vision with action, feelings and sensation, we allow for the creation of something new. To begin your unique relationship with The Eye of Horus, *it is helpful to befriend each stone tablet individually and allow yourself to be touched by each sacred archetype in its turn. Part One is a guide to the text that follows. It includes instructions for the individual divinatory use of the stone tablets and a background to the ideas, meditations and positive thought techniques linked to each one.*

USING THE EYE OF HORUS

Included in *The Eye of Horus* are twenty-five stone tablets designed to be used as an oracle of personal vision, personal development, creativity and spiritual growth. Twenty-three of the stone tablets are linked to a god or goddess of the ancient-Egyptian pantheon. These are powerful human and spiritual archetypes that can teach us much about our true nature. Their essence is timeless and universal. The peoples of the ancient-Egyptian world may not have had the technology that we have today, but they developed a powerful and sophisticated civilization, and they had the same essential needs, fears and concerns as ourselves.

These deities reflect the relationship the Egyptians had with their environment. They reveal human fears about the process of living and dying, a curiosity about the origins of humankind and a perennial concern with the fertility of the land, the harvests and survival. The gods and goddesses were invoked for healing, illumination, success and salvation. Like us, the ancient Egyptians looked to their beliefs to give life meaning and to help make sense of their personal and collective journey through time.

The final two stone tablets are linked to the pyramids and the sphinx: monuments whose images and mysteries still have a powerful impact on us in the modern world. Together, the full set of twenty-five stones is intended to help you make sense of your own personal journey, providing you with a reflection of the world around you and a glimpse of your inner development.

Using this Book

The gods, goddesses or symbols that are linked to the stone tablets are each described in detail in Part Two of this book.

For each stone I have provided 'at a glance' information about the god, goddess or symbol. The name and the four key concepts listed below it are intended to give you the general meaning of the stone tablet. This will help you to determine the overall direction of your readings when you begin to cast and experiment with the stones. The short introduction that follows provides you with accessible information about the symbology linked to the stone.

Then, more detailed background information is provided that will help you to put the god, goddess or symbol into context. Often this includes details about the origins of the god, his or her relationships with other deities, myths and legends and other relevant aspects of the symbology. It is not essential to read this information every time you use the stone tablets but you may find it helpful to look at it occasionally as you deepen your understanding of how to work with these archetypes.

The section following this provides the divinatory meaning for the stone. This is not intended to be a definitive interpretation, but instead is an essential starting point for your own intuitive interpretation of the stone. The Upright text is to be referred to when you pick a stone tablet from the bag and place it in front of you so that the hieroglyphic symbol is the right way up. The Reversed interpretation that follows this is used whenever a stone is placed upside down. You can easily check this by comparing the orientation of the symbol against the picture of the stone that is situated beside the relevant text or within the key at the end of the book *(see page 160)*. The Reversed readings of the stone tablets are not negative ones but tend to be more concerned with the effect that we have upon others, how we are viewed and our current influence within the world at large.

Upright reading

Reversed reading

The divinatory meaning of the stone is then extended further. The section entitled Attributes links the ancient archetypes to modern personality types. This may indicate a person who has a significant effect upon your life for the period of your enquiry or it could be indicative of your own personality at that time. Within this section I suggest links between the archetypes, represented by the gods and goddesses, and the astrological signs of the western horoscope. The Meditation or visualization provided has been designed to highlight and enhance the positive qualities of the archetypes working within you and operating throughout your life. The final section gives seven Positive Affirmations or positive thought techniques for regular use with the stone tablets.

Learning to Use the Stone Tablets

Before you begin, it is important to handle your stones and get used to their feel and look. A good way to do this is to anoint them with oil: you may like to choose a favourite aromatherapy oil, such as lavender or rosemary, blended with almond oil or another suitable carrier. Rub a little onto the stones and allow it to be absorbed into their sandy surface.

When reading the stones, use the written interpretations in Part Two as a guide and build up your own relationship with them, allowing your intuition to add additional layers to their messages. As you digest this information, your readings will improve. Begin by using the stones individually for yourself and, as your confidence grows, progress to the spreads in Part Three.

Place the stones in the draw-string casting bag provided and mix them up so that you are unaware of the exact location of each stone. With the bag in your hand or in front of you, take a moment to close your eyes, breathe deeply and, in your mind, ask the stones to bring you illumination and wisdom. There may be a particular question you have or an area of your life that you would like to focus on at this time, such as your family relationships, your intimate feelings, your health, your career development or your spiritual evolution. If this is the case, think about your question or point of focus for a few seconds.

When you are ready, take a stone tablet, without looking at it first, from the bag and place it in front of you. Notice whether you have positioned it upright or reversed by referring to the key *(see page 160)* which will direct you to the appropriate reading for that stone. Read and use any information that is relevant to your question or your focus of enquiry.

Using the Stone Tablets Individually

There are many ways of using the stone tablets on an individual basis: some suggestions are laid out for you below.

A stone tablet for your day ahead

Choose a stone, unseen, from the bag and refer to the Upright or Reversed reading as appropriate for inspiration and guidance in the day ahead. You may also wish to use the Meditation at some point during the day and the Positive Affirmations, as and when you remember. For those people who regularly begin or end their day with a meditation, this is an excellent way of choosing an appropriate set of positive thoughts or visual images for it.

A stone tablet for the week or month ahead

In a similar manner to choosing a stone for the day, use the Upright or Reversed reading as appropriate for the week or month. Again, you may choose to use the Meditation and Positive Affirmations provided throughout the selected period.

A stone tablet for the year ahead

This can be done at any time of the year but is particularly powerful at the beginning of a new one. For this, it is important to refer to both the Upright and the Reversed readings for the selected stone. It would also be good to use the Meditation and Positive Affirmations periodically, throughout the year. The Attributes section of the stone selected is indicative of the predominant personality traits that you will be expressing, or that you will encounter within others, during your year ahead. It may even suggest that you can harness these facets of your personality to strengthen your spiritual purpose throughout the year and to enhance your ability to be successful.

A stone tablet for specific project or event

Another way to use the stones individually is to pick a stone to guide and inspire each creative project that you undertake. This will give you information about its unique nature and help you to connect with the underlying spiritual purpose that it will fulfil for you and any other people involved. Refer to the Upright or Reversed reading for the stone as appropriate. Stone tablets can be chosen for job interviews, new jobs, courses, promotional events, literary or artistic endeavours, sporting events, business deals and any other projects you feel to be relevant.

A stone tablet to represent a person

You can select a stone tablet to represent a person you are about to meet. Perhaps this is someone you will meet up with socially or someone whom you will encounter at a job interview. For greater clarity and awareness of relationships refer to the Relationship Spread in Part Three *(see pages 142–8)*.

Using the Power of Positive Affirmations

The use of positive thought techniques for health and well-being is not a new concept. Many people have been aware of the power of words and positive visual images for centuries. In recent times, successful self-help books have catered for a growing desire that many people have to learn more about the power of the mind and to become more aware of their inner strengths so that, through these techniques, they can take control of their own healing process.

Complementary therapies have successfully utilized will-power and imagery alongside physical, herbal or auric healing skills. Some areas of standard medical practice are beginning to recognize the value of using positive thought to aid or accelerate healing, and businesses are increasingly training their staff to think for success.

Within *The Eye of Horus* I have included a series of positive affirmations for your use. Each stone tablet has a collection of seven positive statements linked to it. Regular use of these statements can help to bring about a positive change in mental attitude and to stimulate mental, emotional and spiritual evolution. They are declarations of healing intent that can help to bring a deeper understanding of the qualities or archetypes you are exploring.

These affirmations are bold, bright, positively focused statements or ideas that can be used to transform mental attitudes and to aid physical, emotional or spiritual healing. An affirmation is simply a tool that can retrain the mind to think in more positive, constructive and life-enhancing ways. The thoughts, beliefs and attitudes that we hold directly affect the experience we have of our lives. Positive, joyous thoughts are much more likely to create positive, joyful experiences than negative thoughts are. Negative, limiting or rigidly held beliefs can adversely affect our emotional state, our ability to create fulfilling relationships and even our physical health.

Many people are aware of the concept of the self-fulfilling prophecy and the idea that our thoughts affect the life experiences and feelings we create. Our minds are powerful. What we think affects the way we feel about ourselves today and forms the reality of tomorrow. We are more likely to be happy, healthy and prosperous if we are willing to believe that these positive experiences are available to us.

Using positive affirmations on a regular basis can help us to support the spiritual practices, career positions, relationships, exercise programmes, healthy diets and therapies that we have chosen, with brightness and love. What is more, the rhythm and discipline of positivity can help us to deal with and transcend the challenges of life, and to extend the bliss and pleasure of the good times. Affirmations are simple to use and will work for anybody who is willing to persist with them and who is open to experimenting with new, brighter expectations and patterns of thought.

Most people think quite positively for much of the time but there can be areas of old, restrictive or fearful thought that are deeply held or unconscious. These thoughts are often learned, along with some positive ones, very early on in life. The beliefs, attitudes and moods of our parents, or parent figures, were colouring our view of the world from day one. As we grew up, we were also influenced by the beliefs and behaviour of relatives, teachers and other children. Wider patterns of belief would have come to us from our religion, our community and even through the television set or the radio.

Affirmations are used to replace old, learned patterns of thought that no longer serve us, with new, positive ones that do. By affirming positively, we alter our beliefs to support our needs and desires, changing our reality accordingly.

Applying Affirmations in Your Life

The Eye of Horus contains many positive affirmations that have been specially tailored for use with the stone tablets. They have been created to balance and enhance the particular qualities and energies of the archetypes; opening positive channels of thought that may help with health, success, emotional expression and spiritual growth.

There are many ways to use affirmations: some guidelines and suggestions are described below.

Positive affirmations can be written, typed, spoken aloud, sung, chanted or said to yourself in the mirror as well as being repeated over and over in your mind. Many people find that they benefit from filling their homes with affirmational thoughts, perhaps writing or painting them out in bright colours and pasting them on the bathroom mirror, the fridge, on the doors or anywhere else where they will be constantly visible. Be creative and choose ways to use them that work best for you.

Affirmations are wonderful when they are used in conjunction with meditation or physical exercise. Choosing one or two affirmations that are easy to remember and repeating them silently to yourself in your mind with the rhythm of your breath or in time to the repetition of a familiar exercise can help them to become second nature. You may even repeat affirmations in your mind as you walk, pacing them out with every step that you take.

Affirmations can easily be recorded for you to listen to while you are meditating, relaxing, having a bath, pottering around your home, travelling to work or at any other time you choose. You could make a tape by getting a trusted friend or family member to speak your chosen series of positive thoughts into a tape recorder. Ask them to include your name from time to time so that it is as personally tailored as possible. Even more powerful would be a recording of your own voice speaking the affirmations: again put your own name into some of the positive statements. For example, '*I, David, am passionate about my ideas,*' or '*Susan, you are always motivated and inspired.*' You may choose to build up a collection of tapes to use over and over again.

Although it is wonderful to set aside some special time every day, or every couple of days, to focus on your affirmations, you do not have to view them as yet another task to fit into your busy schedule. The best way to use them is to make them an integral part of your life. You could affirm on your way to and from work, while you are cooking the dinner, while you are doing the housework or going through your morning routine. Perhaps the best times for you to do affirmations are those last few minutes at night just before you go to sleep and those first few minutes in the morning when you are still waking up. These are times when your mind is receptive and when you can influence your night's rest or the mood of your day ahead. After a time you may wake up with the positive thoughts already there in your mind, repeating themselves with brightness and clarity to welcome you to the day.

Some of the best affirmations to use are those that run contrary to your current beliefs or differ greatly from what is presently real and true for you. For example, if you are sick or unwell then it may seem strange to affirm *'I am always in perfect health.'* However, it will probably be one of the most appropriate positive statements to practice. Of course, you do need to recognize what is happening to your body and make appropriate choices about treatments; although while you are doing this, the exercise of affirming for health will support your healing process and help the treatments that you have chosen to work.

The more you use positive affirmations, the more they can work for you. Sometimes it is good to have a few favourite affirmations that you will always remember wherever you are while frequently introducing your mind to new ones that address a particular need. You can never have too many positive thoughts, but, when you are first introducing your mind to them, it is perhaps better to have a few that you will be able to memorize and use rather than an endless list that can be easily forgotten.

Remember, affirmations are meant to be fun. Play with them, experiment with them and find ways to use them that are entertaining for you.

Creating Your Own Affirmations

After using the affirmations I have devised for use with the stones, you may wish to experiment with creating some of your own. Here are some guidelines to help you:

- Affirmations often work best when they are relatively short and easy to remember.
- Affirmations need to be phrased in the present tense. For example, *'I now create ...'* (present simple tense) or *'I am always ...'* (present continuous tense). If you affirm for something as if it is already true for you, then your mind can more readily make the changes that will alter your experience of life. However, if you affirm that something is *going* to happen or that it *will* happen, then you are creating it in the future, and that is where it will stay, constantly out of reach. *'In three weeks I will be ...'* will always stay three weeks away.
- In most cases affirmations need to be positively focused on your desired outcome, rather than on the situations or conditions that you want to release. For example, *'I am healthy and relaxed'* is a much more effec-

tive affirmation than *'I am never sick or tense.'* The latter will keep your attention unduly focused on the negative outcome, continuing to make it a reality in your life.

• Your negative or limiting thoughts are the raw material for creating positive affirmations. Each of these negative thoughts contains the foundation for positive change and growth. *'My life will never change for the better'* can become *'My life always changes for the better.'*

• For anyone wishing to explore the use of affirmations, positive thought techniques and other aspects of self-healing, there are many excellent books available *(see Further Reading, page 158)*.

Using the Power of Meditation and Visualization

Visualization is the use of mental images to create the experiences we choose to have in our lives. By using the power of our minds, we can daydream away stress, create calm and peace, prevent illness, promote good health, awaken our psychic or intuitive abilities, accelerate our spiritual development and strengthen our personal growth.

Many people have already discovered that the power of creative daydreams has a miraculous effect on their home environment, their career, their finances and their relationships. To change your world, you begin by changing the way you picture it; the rest follows naturally.

Visualization and all positive thought techniques work directly on the most important relationship of all: the relationship we have with ourselves. How else can we create health, love and success in our lives if we do not see ourselves as healthy, lovable and successful?

Within *The Eye of Horus*, I have created twenty-five meditations that utilize visualization techniques. All of these meditations strengthen and enhance the positive qualities of the archetypes linked to the stones and sow seeds for the imagination. Some awaken psychic or intuitive abilities; others are concerned with healing or personal evolution; all are intended to stimulate a new awareness of our essential nature. The use of visualization is a powerful way of accessing innate abilities and providing a key to positive changes.

Setting the Scene

For all of the meditation or visualization exercises included in *The Eye of Horus* the ideal environment would be a safe, quiet place that is warm and comfortable. Minimize possible distractions by unplugging telephones and ensuring that other people will not disturb you. You can use music in the background if it helps you to relax but make sure that it is calming and melodic and without lyrics that would fight for your attention.

Lie down on your back in a comfortable position or sit with your back properly supported, making sure that your feet are firmly planted on the floor. It is preferable to keep your arms and legs, hands and feet uncrossed, ensuring that your body is open and receptive. Remember to breathe deeply and slowly throughout your visualization and make sure that your body will be warm as you relax.

Once you are familiar with the images and techniques suggested within the book, you may wish to practise meditating in many different situations – sitting on a bus, for instance – but the scenario described above is the easiest. However, remember that these techniques are not to be used while driving a car or in any other situation where you need all of your concentration.

It is not important to follow every detail of the visualization exercises exactly. It would not be very relaxing for you to feel that you have to work hard to get all of the details correct and in the right order. Just read them through a couple of times to familiarize yourself with their essence before settling down and trusting your mind to take care of the images for you. If it helps, then make a tape recording of your voice guiding you through the visualizations or, alternatively, you could ask a trusted friend to talk you through them.

Some people have a natural ability to think in pictures while for others it comes with practice. Regardless of how your mind works, your intention is much more important than your capacity to have strong visual images. Just holding the concept or the idea of the picture in your mind is enough for these techniques to work for you.

Giving your mind the freedom to play is more beneficial than trying hard to be absolutely accurate. Remember, the more you play with the visualizations in this book, the easier they become. Please feel free to adapt any of the images to your changing needs or special preferences; after a while you may find your imagination automatically extends and enhances them.

PART TWO

THE STONE TABLETS

'The Eye of Horus is your protection; it spreads its protection over you ... The Eye of Horus comes intact and shining like Re in the horizon; it covers up the powers of Seth who would possess it.'

THE ANCIENT EGYPTIAN BOOK OF THE DEAD

True protection does not come from preparing ourselves to attack or defend. Protection of all that is sacred to us comes from developing our awareness and honing our personal 'magic' so that we may be effective in our lives and in the world. When we develop a positive, loving intention, a trust in our own abilities and a powerful vision of our way forward then we are truly protected. This section is a guide to the sacred archetypes linked to the stone tablets. Allow these gods, goddesses and sacred symbols to shower you with their gifts of positive intention, vision and awareness. Let The Eye of Horus *be your protection.*

SYMBOLS AND HIEROGLYPHS

The twenty-five stone tablets included in *The Eye of Horus* bear images that have been drawn from the symbology of the gods and goddesses and from the hieroglyphic writing of the ancient Egyptians. Some of the images chosen are directly related to the image of the god or goddess as depicted in full illustrations on temple walls and elsewhere. One example of this is the head of the god Seth, a composite beast, which has been chosen to represent him on the stone tablet within the collection.

The head of Seth representing the god on the stone tablet

The perfume jar representing the cat goddess Bastet

Other images are drawn from the wider symbology of the god or goddess concerned but are also to be found amongst the characters of hieroglyphic writing. An example of this is the perfume jar of the cat goddess Bastet, which is also one of the three characters that appears in her name when it is written in hieroglyphs. The names of the gods and goddesses, when written in hieroglyphs, are sometimes spelt out phonetically, sometimes represented by a single determinative symbol and sometimes by a combination of phonetic and determinative characters.

Traditionally, the hieroglyphs of ancient Egypt could be read side to side, from left to right or from right to left. The latter was more common but there are surviving examples of both types, as well as examples of hieroglyphic writing that was intended to be read upwards or downwards in columns. The key to the orientation of the characters lies in the direction they are facing. A head or a figure facing to the left was intended to be read from left to right, whereas if it was facing to the right, the reverse would have been true.

The stone tablets created here for *The Eye of Horus* are designed to be read from left to right. The symbols and images that are not depicted facing head on are looking to the left. Note that in the case of the stone of Khepri, the god shown below, it is this orientation that indicates whether the stone has been drawn upright or reversed.

The stone of Khepri drawn upright. Note that the scarab is facing to the left.

GEB

God of the Earth

— Ecology —

— Nourishment —

— Parental Judgement —

— Authority —

The god Geb is the embodiment of the earth. In some depictions he is seated, while in others he reclines with one arm to the sky and the other to the ground. He is the father of the gods and is linked to the throne of Egypt in various ways, investing the rightful heir with the authority to rule. As brother and husband of the sky goddess Nut, he is sometimes shown with her. As Geb reclines, Nut arches above him. Sometimes he is aroused and sometimes he is impregnating her. Geb provides the fruits of the earth to nourish and sustain, and it is said that barley grows from his ribs. The hieroglyph of his name is the symbol for a white-fronted goose. His colours are the greens of lush vegetation.

The Creation Myth of Heliopolis

According to the mythology of ancient Egypt, before the creation there was Nu, an ocean of water without limit that filled the darkness. The waters of Nu are symbolic of the non-existence before and beyond life that was imagined by the intellectuals at Heliopolis. Nu was seen as a constant presence that continued to be in evidence even after the advent of creation. There was a common fear that Nu would smash through the sky and drown the earth into non-existence once more.

The creator god was Atum, who was believed to have risen out of the waters of Nu. He was seen as a self-created deity, a sun god, who stood upon a raised mound and contained within himself all of the forces of nature. Although he was essentially viewed as a male god, he also embodied the feminine principle. From his semen he gave birth to the twin god and goddess, Shu and Tefnut; Shu is the god of the air and Tefnut is the goddess of moisture. It was from the union of air and moisture in the form of this brother and sister that the earth god Geb and his sister Nut were born.

The Fertility of Egypt

Geb is representative of the earth as a whole and in particular he was the embodiment of the land of Egypt. He is symbolic of the richness and abundance of the earth as well as aspects of nature that were feared. He is often coloured green, with barley or other lush vegetation growing from his body. His fertility is highlighted by depictions that include his phallus or show him beneath the sky goddess Nut as they copulate. He was sometimes feared because the dead were buried in the earth and because of the earthquakes and eruptions that were associated with him.

It is interesting to note that Geb, as god of the earth, and Nut, as goddess of the sky, provide a model for the world that is contrary to the dominant beliefs of India, Europe and the Americas. In these cultural traditions, the earth is the feminine principle and the sky is the male principle. However, there is a universal understanding that the union of the two brings forth life.

Geb and Government

Geb is often portrayed as a figure of paternal authority. He is a judge and a governor as well as a source of abundant fertility. In the contest for the throne of Egypt between his murderous son Seth and his avenging grandson Horus, some sources tell of Geb being the god who presided over the tribunal, while others attribute that role to the sun god Re.

Geb was seen to pass his earthly authority to his eldest son Osiris; then, following the murder of Osiris by Seth, he bestowed his authority on his grandson Horus. The final figure of this lineage was seen to be the human king of Egypt whose role granted him immortality. Geb was thus said to be the father of the gods, and the king was the rightful heir of Geb.

GEB IN A READING

Upright

If you have chosen this stone tablet in a reading then it is time to look at how you are nourishing and sustaining yourself. Are you providing for your needs or are you living a life that is out of balance with your physical, emotional or spiritual rhythms? This is a time for re-examining your diet and making sure that you are eating fresh, simple food that will keep you healthy rather than over-dosing on junk food or skipping meals entirely. It is also a time for pacing yourself, regulating your sleeping patterns and taking regular exercise. Extremes of any kind are to be avoided; you will gain the greatest pleasure from simplicity and moderation.

The stone of Geb augurs a period of richness. It represents the natural abundance that comes with respecting your body, your humanity and the environment you live in. Imagine yourself to be like a plant with its roots in the earth. We all need roots to allow for new growth and expansion. It helps to have a stable home life and personal space for safe retreat, but even if this is not available then you still have the potential to create a firm foundation of inner security.

Ask yourself, *'Are my roots embedded in rich, fertile ground or are they planted in earth that will not sustain them?'* This is a time for you to choose between the dry, stony ground of negative thinking, emotional dishonesty and non-supportive relationships, and the fertile earth of positive thought (the minerals), honest emotional expression (the waters) and stable friendships (the substance of the earth). The richness of Geb is available to you, but only you can choose to plant your roots where they will be nourished and where your growth and development will be supported.

Reversed

If this stone tablet is reversed then you may find yourself providing the rich, fertile ground that sustains the dreams and desires of others. Your presence creates the stability for them to grow and thrive. This is a positive role for you. Everyone concerned will benefit greatly from your service, yourself included. However, if someone is expecting you to take responsibility for their misdeeds, shortcomings or inability to act, then you would be advised to assess your situation very carefully. Does your leadership and guidance rob anyone of their need to stabilize themselves? Are you protecting others from the consequences of their own shortcomings? As long as you are clear about your role and continue to exercise sound judgement then your influence will provide an abundant harvest for everyone to enjoy.

This is also a time for reviewing your relationship with paternal authority. Do you need to heal your relationship with your father? Do you need to learn how to be a stable parent for your own children or provide sound judgement for younger family members, junior employees or anyone else who looks to you for authority and leadership?

Despite the roles we take, we all have our own hopes, fears and desires. Remember to be loving and compassionate to everyone, regardless of whether they appear to be in authority above you or whether they see you as the figure of authority.

Attributes

If this stone tablet represents a person who has come into your life then they will be a figure of authority who commands respect through their display of seniority, sound judgement and steadfastness. This person is trustworthy, reliable and honest. Their presence helps to validate a project or give weight to an approach. You are likely to benefit from their wisdom and they may furnish you with the endorsement or approval that you require for success. Alternatively, this is a person who campaigns for environmental issues or political stability. In western astrology the qualities of Geb most directly relate to the sign of Capricorn.

Meditation

Close your eyes, breathe deeply and relax. For this visualization it is best to sit upright, with your feet firmly planted on the floor in front of you. As you breathe, imagine that you have roots growing from the centre of your feet and visualize them expanding rapidly, moving downwards and branching out in all directions. Picture these roots easily penetrating the floor beneath you; quickly finding their way to the earth even if they have to travel through many storeys or dig deep through concrete foundations. If you are outside, just see them going deeper and deeper into the earth. Once your roots are in place, the earth sends an abundance of healing energy through them to stabilize and protect you. See your roots drinking in this energy and drawing it up into your body. Remain in this position for as long as is comfortable and complete the meditation by picturing your roots contracting again, leaving you strong and secure.

POSITIVE AFFIRMATIONS

The earth sustains me.
I am guided by the divine father.
My life is rich, fertile and abundant.
I bring healing to the earth and receive healing for myself.
I am always supported by my environment.
I am the authority in my life.
I am stable and secure.

NUT

Goddess of the Sky

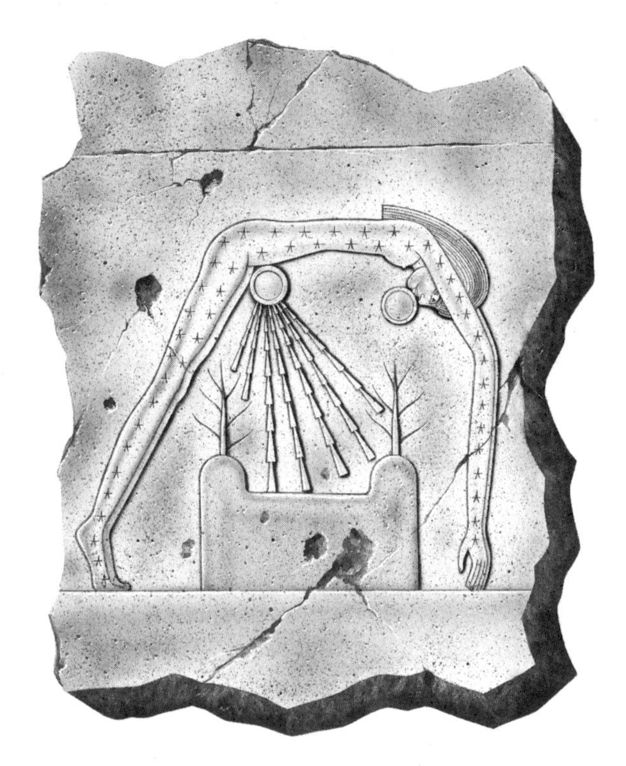

— Mystery —

— Firmament —

— Sustenance —

— Laughter —

The goddess Nut is the wife and sister of Geb and the mother of Isis, Osiris, Seth and Nephthys. As the goddess of the sky, she is often depicted with her body stretched out over the earth, her hands and feet at the cardinal points. She is the firmament that protects the world from the amorphous chaos beyond, and as such she maintains all that is in existence. Sometimes Nut is depicted as a sky cow and often she has stars on her body or her dress. Indeed, she was sometimes described as the 'mistress of the heavenly bodies' and she was thought to draw stars into her mouth and expel them from her womb in a repeating cycle. Her colours are the indigo of the night sky and the silver lights of the stars.

The Image of Nut

Many depictions of the goddess Nut show her side on with her body extended over the earth. From this perspective she appears to have her hands close together and her two feet a short distance apart from each other. However, the true Egyptian view of this goddess was of a figure stretched out at width as well as at length so that each hand and foot rested upon one of the cardinal points of the earth, to the North, South, East and West. In some pictures she is supported by her father Shu, god of the air, who stands below her with his arms raised, like some ancient-Egyptian Atlas.

The hieroglyph for Nut consists of three symbols. Firstly the sky or heaven symbol that is indicative of the goddess. This is a simplified depiction of Nut's body stretched out across the earth. Because it is a flat, two-dimensional image, the sky hieroglyph looks a little like the side view of a table. Secondly, there is a jar or bowl symbol and, completing the picture, is the hieroglyph for a bread loaf. These are the symbols that represent the goddess on the stone of Nut.

Like many Egyptian goddesses, Nut was associated with the cow, a beast that was viewed as a source of nurture and nourishment. Her depiction as a cow indicated great maternal strength and benign wisdom. The sky was a protective mother to the mortals living upon the earth and her body acted as a shield above them. Even the potentially frightening rumble of thunder was seen by some as benign: it was the laughter of Nut.

The Heavenly Bodies

Nut had a special relationship with the sun and the stars. She was thought to swallow the stars in the morning and give birth to the sun. During the day, the sun would travel across her body and, in the evening, this too would be swallowed as the stars issued forth from her womb. This image was likened to a sow swallowing and then giving birth to her piglets. In her form as a cow and as a woman she was often pictured with stars upon her body. As a sow she could be depicted suckling her 'children'.

This daily cycle of death and rebirth created an obvious connection between Nut and the funerary rites of the Egyptians. The tomb chamber and sarcophagus of a king or noble would often be decorated with images of Nut or of the stars. The dead king was sometimes thought to dwell within the sky goddess, and Nut became thought of as the coffin of the heavens.

Mother of the Gods

With her brother and husband Geb, Nut conceived the gods and goddesses of the Osiran myths. Geb, the earth god, is often shown reclining below her with one arm downwards and one arm raised, while his phallus is often elevated to the sky. Osiris and Isis, the first born male and female children, became the original governors of Egypt. Their younger siblings are Seth and Nephthys. Seth, the god of destruction who usurped his brother, is said to have ripped himself savagely from the womb of Nut.

NUT IN A READING

Upright

If you have chosen this stone tablet in a reading then you are being reminded to expect the best and move beyond the basic survival fears we learn in early childhood. The sky is not going to fall on your head and your life will not be engulfed in chaos unless you actively invite it with your negative or fearful thoughts. For many of us, the choice to live our lives as spiritual beings on a path of human development comes with some resistance. As children, the instinct for survival is strong but our resistance to life, combined with the fears, negative beliefs and limitations that we learn from our parents, has an effect on everything that we experience. If we are fearful of life then we grow up to expect disaster and we make ourselves more available to illness, problematic relationships and financial struggle.

The stone of Nut augurs a time of moving beyond the mentality of struggle and into the joy, fun and the expansiveness of being alive. By changing the way that we view the world, we can give up trying to survive and instead learn how to thrive. Nut brings us universal possibilities and limitless opportunities when we make ourselves available for her bountiful gifts. Regularly tell yourself that it is safe to be alive. Begin to make friends with the uncertainty that we all face. Nothing is fixed; the world is constantly changing. Rather than waste energy trying to control every experience, train yourself to expect the best and trust yourself to handle anything that life brings you. If there is thunder in the air, it is our choice to view it as the rumble of impending disaster when in reality it is just the laughter of Nut.

Nut reminds us that the world will sustain us if we allow it to. We all have the capacity to experience prosperity, well-being, good relationships with kindred souls and fulfilling career opportunities. The whole world is available to you now. The sky is the limit. There is no turning back. It is up to you to embrace the mystery and uncertainty of your life and take the next step forward. This is the planet of your dreams.

Reversed

If this stone is reversed then your influence inspires other people to move beyond struggle mentality and learn to enjoy the mystery and uncertainty of life. Your presence reminds others that there is a universe full of possibilities still to be explored; life is a bountiful adventure. Nut is a mother and protector, and your influence may be parental and nurturing too. It may be that you can see the latent gifts and talents your 'children' or protégés have hidden within them and you know how to awaken those gifts so that they may shine like the stars. However, it is not always essential to put your energy into their progress. By being yourself and by living your dream, you awaken others to the possibilities for advancement, spiritual growth and success. Alternatively, you may be teaching other people the value of humour and reminding them that sometimes the best we can do is surrender to the process of life, laugh at our limitations and trust the divine. Life moves on, day follows night and night follows day. We are ultimately too big to get caught up in petty arguments or get bogged down with minor details. In reaching for the cardinal points, Nut also reaches into the future and she knows that the future is glorious for all who are willing to see the bigger picture.

Attributes

If this stone tablet represents a person then they will be fun, friendly, enthusiastic and full of ideas; always on the lookout for new challenges, new inventions and stimulating relationships. She or he could appear to be rebellious, constantly challenging convention and pushing against petty bureaucracy. However, while being dynamic and expansive, they have an underlying need for order and stability too. They are often quite conservative but this is not immediately apparent. The qualities of Nut most directly relate to the sign of Aquarius in western astrology.

Meditation

Close your eyes, breathe deeply and relax. Visualize yourself flying through the night sky, free and light, protected by the love of Nut as you travel through her domain. Imagine all limitations and restrictions dropping away as you stretch and glide. Invite new sources of inspiration and joy into your life. Keep your mind open to new ideas, energy and opportunities. Picture the stars shining on you and imagine that with every breath you fill your lungs with fresh, clean air and radiant starlight. Starlight brightens your heart and your circulation carries oxygen and the healing inspiration of the stars to every part of your body. Finally, picture yourself placing your feet firmly on the ground. You are filled with inspiration and are able to put new ideas into action. Allow your talents to shine.

POSITIVE AFFIRMATIONS

I evoke the healing power of laughter.
I fulfil my divine purpose.
I touch the sky with my dreams.
I expand my horizons.
I easily see the bigger picture of my life.
My present sustains me, the future invites me.
I am positive and optimistic.

OSIRIS

Lord of the Underworld

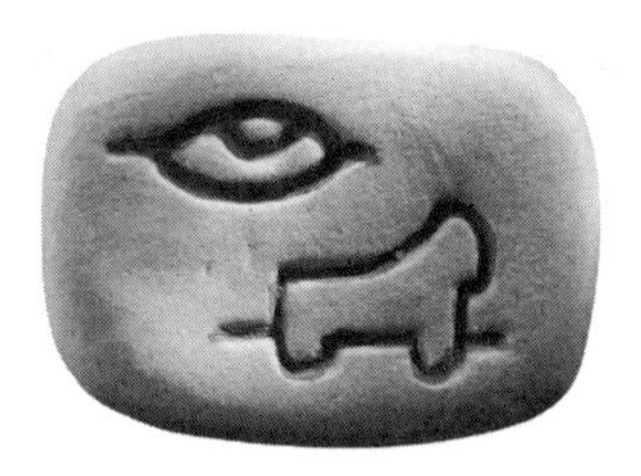

— Might —

— Universal Power —

— Fertility —

— Continuing Life —

The god Osiris is the first-born son of Geb and Nut. He is usually depicted as a mummified figure holding the sceptres of kingship. His conical crown sits on a base of ram's horns and bears plumes on each side. The hieroglyph of his name is comprised of a symbol for an eye and a royal carrying chair. Osiris is a universal god who is capable of absorbing the qualities of other divinities into his own personality. He is linked to the growing and harvesting of crops, and, as such, represents the development of civilization. However, he is mainly associated with the continuation of life after death and the enduring light of the spirit. Osiris presided over the Egyptian underworld, which is called 'Duat'. His colours are white and green.

Osiris the King

Osiris is said to have ruled over pre-dynastic Egypt with his sister Isis at his side as his queen. His rule on Earth was a golden age of prosperity, with the forces of nature firmly under his control. The Earthly reign of Osiris was ended abruptly when he was murdered by his brother, Seth, whose attempt to usurp his elder's position was initially successful. The right to the throne of Osiris was eventually claimed by his son, Horus. The Pharaohs asserted their prerogative to rule by proclaiming to be the son of Osiris. They became the living embodiment of Horus with divine power bestowed on them by their father in the underworld.

After his death, Osiris became the sovereign of the underworld. For the ancient Egyptians, his reign of the underworld symbolized the continuation of life after death. When the mortal rulers of Egypt reached their deaths, they ceased to be seen as the embodiment of Horus and instead became Osiris, King of Duat. This transition assured them of immortality and a continuing role of leadership. They could now give orders from the throne of Osiris.

The Murder of Osiris

Accounts of the murder of Osiris vary. Some tell of the god being killed on the banks of the river at Nedyet. According to this version, Seth begins his attack on Osiris in the land of Gahesty and slaughters him at Nedyet where he succumbs to his demise only after some resistance. Yet, in other accounts, Seth tricks Osiris by enticing him to step into a chest and locking him in. Once secure, the chest containing Osiris is thrown into the Nile and the god drowns. This version is perhaps symbolic of the flooding of the Nile which fertilized the land, allowing for new crop growth and a good harvest.

Later stories tell of Seth dismembering Osiris and cutting his body into fourteen parts that were then scattered throughout Egypt. With the help of her sister Nephthys, Isis searched for the body and, on discovering and reassembling the pieces, she preserved it for his life in the underworld.

Continuing Life

The role of Osiris as a god of agriculture comes from the story of his death and rebirth. His murder and resurrection draws a parallel to crops, which are harvested only to be reseeded and given new life. There is even a reference to the murder of Osiris that likens the god to barley being threshed. Symbolically, Seth is threshing the barley as he cuts the body of Osiris into pieces. Osiris represented elemental harmony, lush vegetation and fertility, in contrast to Seth who was god of the desert and chaotic elemental forces. It is possible that the continuing life of Osiris gave the Egyptians hope of new crop growth and survival after a season of dry or stormy weather, as well as symbolizing their belief in life beyond death.

The Egyptian fear of death spawned a link between Osiris and the sun god Re. As twin souls, they would ensure that the underworld was illuminated by solar light.

OSIRIS IN A READING

Upright

If you have chosen this stone tablet in a reading then be aware that this is a time of renewal and continuing life. Often we view the conclusion of a cycle, the end of an era or the completion of a project with a sense of fear or dread. Ahead of us there is the void of the unknown, paths that have yet to be chosen or new projects that offer an uncertain future. Take heart and view the next chapter of your life with joy, trust and positive anticipation. The stone of Osiris represents both the end and the beginning of any cycle as well as symbolizing the ongoing journey that we all take towards new life, new growth and greater awareness. There is much to be learned and much that we can gain if we believe that it is safe for us to take the next step forward.

When we begin something new we may feel uncertain of our identity. Established roles, jobs and relationships give us a secure position to operate from; we know what is expected of us and we often do not feel that we have to prove our worth. Stepping into something new, however, can leave us feeling vulnerable and unsure of ourselves. Sometimes the experience and confidence that we have developed over the years seem to evaporate and we are left feeling like a child on his or her first day at school. While we can learn to develop a degree of confidence that will sustain us through most things, it is important to recognize that there are many gifts to be had from a period of uncertainty. When feeling unsure of ourselves we can reject our rigid thinking and can make new choices that may bring unexpected benefits.

The stone of Osiris augurs a time of fertility. Life is rich with opportunities, personal growth is available to you and, at this moment, you are particularly open to success. Remember that nothing valuable can truly be destroyed: nothing that you learn is ever lost and no act of kindness is ever forgotten. Everything of value that you have ever done or experienced will continue to enrich your life and ensure that your future is blessed with good fortune.

Reversed

If this stone tablet is reversed then your influence brings a sense of new or continuing life to others. You are viewed as a powerful force whose example inspires other people to trust themselves and get on with the process of living. Your presence engenders the hope that new horizons are available to everyone after periods of challenge or sudden change. Your impact is most pronounced when you are committed to your own personal development rather than tied up in trying to transform other people. There is no benefit in moulding others to your will; instead you need to trust them to make their own choices. Be assured that by being as self-motivated and joyful as you can be, you are having a positive, motivational effect on those around you.

Osiris reversed also indicates a time for letting go of relationships that no longer support you. By moving on you will liberate yourself and others to create new life.

Attributes

If this stone tablet represents a person then they will radiate stability, confidence and a strong sense of personal power. This is a naturally positive and self-assured individual who has transcended and survived their own life challenges. He or she has learned through experience that they can handle most obstacles that life throws in their path and they know how to turn their weaknesses into strengths. This person still has her or his own hopes and fears like anyone else but they have developed a degree of freedom from self-doubt and they are able to enjoy the ongoing adventure of life. The qualities attributed by the stone of Osiris most directly relate to the signs of Sagittarius, Leo and Virgo in western astrology.

Meditation

Close your eyes, breathe deeply and relax. Picture your body surrounded by white light and visualize yourself walking past fields of wheat and barley. Begin by seeing the crops as green and tender, and then picture them ripening, speeding up time in your imagination so that they can reach golden maturity at an accelerated rate. As the crops mature, imagine that your current hopes, dreams, goals and fears come to a safe and satisfactory completion. As the crops are reaped, see yourself harvesting the rewards of your present relationships, projects and choices before moving on to better things. The white light protects you and helps to cleanse you of any thoughts, feelings and life choices that do not serve your highest good.

When you are ready, see the fields being reseeded. Each seed is protected by a coating of white light that will ensure safe and positive growth in your life. All new choices you make will come to prosperous fruition.

POSITIVE AFFIRMATIONS

My life gets better all the time.
My body radiates life force, energy and vitality.
I have the right to live and thrive.
My life is abundantly rich and prosperous.
It is safe for me to learn new things.
My life is filled with new opportunities.
I move on to greater glory and greater rewards.

ISIS

Mother of Magic and Majesty

— Devotion —

— Magical Skills —

— Motherhood —

— Loyalty —

The goddess Isis is an embodiment of the Divine Mother, just as the Hindu goddesses Kali and Durga are within Indian culture and the Virgin Mary is within many interpretations of the Christian faith. She is often represented by a hieroglyphic throne symbol that indicates her royal bearing or her influence over the kingship of Egypt. The stone tablet for Isis reflects this. Sometimes she is seen to wear a crown of cow horns to represent her maternal power; legends also have her taking the form of a cow or a sow for similar reasons. Isis is the daughter of the earth god Geb and the sky goddess Nut. She is the sister and consort of Osiris, who ruled over the earth with her at his side until his demise. The colour associated with Isis is bright blue.

The Power of Isis

Born of Geb and Nut, Isis is the sister of Osiris, Seth and Nephthys. The power of Isis comes from her own special qualities of guile, wisdom, compassion and tenacity as much as from her lineage. There are many stories of her magical gifts and her skill in applying them. Isis foresees the murder of Osiris by Seth and, after his death, she tirelessly reassembles the dismembered parts of his body. Using her magic, she resurrects Osiris momentarily so that they may copulate. In some depictions she hovers above him in the form of a kite or sparrow hawk as she is impregnated.

Isis is the epitome of devotion. During the life of her brother and husband Osiris, she is devoted to assisting him in the government of Egypt. After his murder by Seth, her devotion to Osiris is displayed through the mourning of his loss and her resourcefulness in conceiving a son, Horus, to take his father's place as king. Like anyone who is devoted to their family, Isis displays great courage and commitment in protecting her own kind and is even swayed by family loyalty when presented with an opportunity to kill her murderous brother Seth. This arises during one episode in the contest between Seth and Horus for the kingship of Egypt. Both gods take the form of hippopotomi and Isis is able to harpoon her brother while he is submerged under water. In a moment of compassion, she puts aside her own desire for her son Horus to be victorious and relents, using her magic to draw the harpoon from Seth's body.

Mother of the Pharaoh

The throne symbol that represents Isis is indicative of how the goddess herself embodied and epitomized the throne of Egypt. In protecting her son Horus and assisting him to take his rightful place as king, Isis was seen as instrumental in bestowing the Pharaohs of ancient Egypt with their divine right to rule. In her position as the mother of Horus, she was also the symbolic mother of all the Pharaohs. The ruler of Egypt was said to suckle milk from the breasts of his mother, Isis, and indeed the image of Isis seated upon a throne with the young Horus sitting on her lap, suckling at her breast, is a common one.

The Magic of Isis

In addition to symbolizing the feminine power of the queen, the mother and the female consort, Isis is representative of the high priestess and the healer. Her special abilities as a magician set her apart from many other gods and goddesses in the Egyptian pantheon. She is the archetype of the autonomous feminine principle that exists within us all, and which is equal and complementary to the male principle rather than subordinate to it.

The magical healing skills of Isis include prayers for the curing of childhood ailments, bites and scalds. In rituals of healing, the person suffering from fever, burns or poison would take the role of the young Horus and Isis would be called upon to remedy the ills of her sick child.

ISIS IN A READING

Upright

If you have chosen this stone tablet in a reading then take heart because you will be well supported in whatever you are choosing to do. If you have been devoting yourself to a special cause, your career advancement or a vocational enterprise, then it is important that you trust yourself and trust the forces that are at work in the world around you. Despite the changes of fortune that you have experienced and the challenges that you have faced, your life is on course. You are taking your rightful place in the world and fulfilling your divine purpose.

Perhaps you are devoting yourself to someone as a loyal partner, lover, parent, teacher or colleague. This is a time when your loyalty to another person will bring great benefits for all concerned. Be true to your ideals, be true to your goals, but most of all be true to your heart. It is your love and care of yourself and others that give you the most joy.

It is essential at this time that you remain flexible and adapt to each new situation that you find yourself in. Isis was able to adopt many forms and disguises to fulfil her role as divine mother, wife and magician. In the same way, you have the ability to assume roles that are pertinent to the many different people and experiences that you are destined to encounter. You can be a devoted friend and confidant, a tough negotiator, a creative genius, an efficient executive, a nurturing parent or a passionate lover. You have a million other facets to your personality too, as long as you are loyal to your heart and to your highest healing potential.

Above all, the stone of Isis augurs magical changes of consciousness; so relax and allow yourself the happiness that you seek. It is possible that your skills as a healer, a psychic or a counsellor are growing rapidly, or that you are waking up to your unique qualities and gifts. Look at yourself closely and acknowledge how beautiful, special and resourceful you truly are.

Reversed

If this stone tablet is reversed then you are encouraged to use your wit and guile to shelter or protect another person. Is there a member of your family or a friend who can only succeed with your help, insight and protection at this time? Whom can you bring assistance to without disabling their autonomy or obstructing their ability to choose for themselves? You could be an angel of mercy who provides others with a shoulder to cry on or a 'fixer' who works behind the scenes to make dreams come true. You may even be an advocate or a diplomat who promotes the rights of other people, speaking for them when they are not always able to do so for themselves.

If you are a parent, then choosing Isis upright or reversed indicates that your parenting skills are growing and blossoming. Even those of us who choose not to have children still have the potential to develop positive parenting skills in our lives. We can learn to nurture our friends, colleagues or clients; choosing a social position or professional role that will allow us to express our gift for caring.

Attributes

If this stone tablet represents a person who has come into your life then it will be someone whose maternal sense of loyalty and devotion brings you confidence, strength of purpose and stability. This could be your own mother or someone who is a mother to many. However, do not be fooled by appearances: the energy of the Divine Mother can radiate from women and men alike. Children, too, can bring divine parenting to their elders. This person offers magical solutions to problems and she or he brings the kind of healing that only comes with a mother's touch. The qualities of Isis are most directly linked to the sign of Cancer in western astrology.

Meditation

Close your eyes, breathe deeply and relax. In your mind ask Isis to heal and protect you. Tell yourself, *'I am willing to receive the healing of the Divine Mother.'* Picture yourself surrounded by a light of bright, sky blue and imagine all physical, mental and emotional toxins safely being released from your body, drawn into the light before dissolving completely. All areas of disease, pain, disharmony or negative thought are instantly transformed by the light of Isis.

Visualize the blue healing ray of Isis continuing to heal you over the next few days. This force makes you magnetic to people, experiences and situations that can contribute to your well-being. At the same time, picture Isis surrounding you with soft wings of protection and imagine yourself cushioned by a feeling of warmth and gentleness. The wings of Isis touch your heart and shelter every part of you, comforting you and keeping you safe.

POSITIVE AFFIRMATIONS

I am loyal to my needs, dreams and desires.
I am blessed and cherished always.
I easily heal myself and nourish my creative power.
I am guided by the divine mother.
I devote myself to the creation of happiness and success.
My magical influence creates divine harmony around me.
I am magnetic to the love and care that I need.

SETH

King of Chaos

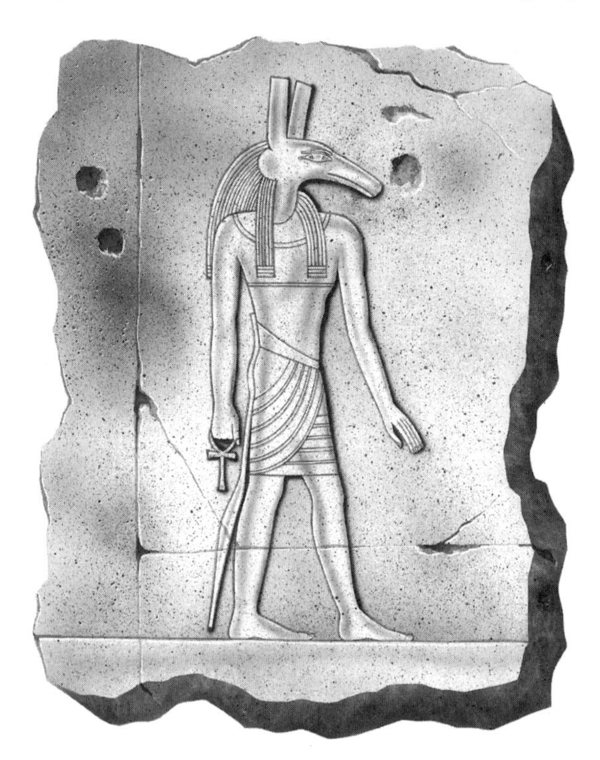

— Rebellion —

— Destruction —

— Rivalry —

— Sovereignty —

The god Seth is the brother of Osiris, Isis and Nephthys. Born of Geb and Nut he is of the royal line and some Pharaohs associated themselves and their right to rule with his name rather than with the name of Horus and Osiris. Seth is generally depicted as a humanoid creature with the curving muzzle and tail of a beast, and two appendages jutting out from the top of his head. Legend paints Seth as a destructive, chaotic god. He is the murderer of his brother Osiris and he represents the rebellious, untamed forces within human and elemental nature that were feared by many. He is associated with stormy weather and cloudiness as well as various animals such as the hippopotamus, the crocodile and the boar. His colour is red.

Seth the King

Seth was said to be 'great in strength', an epithet indicative of the power that was attributed to this god and of his central position in the culture and beliefs of many ancient Egyptians. In some regions, Seth was the sovereign god and was the deity linked with the right to kingship. The story of Seth's murderous act upon his brother Osiris, and his subsequent contest with his nephew Horus for the throne of Egypt, is associated by some scholars with the process of rationalizing the supremacy of one set of belief systems over another.

Within Egypt there were many different factions, each with their own belief systems and chief deities. The popularity, political correctness and expansion of some cults may have been based on associating one god with another or giving gods relationships that explain their positions within each new political or religious order. Seth may not have always been a chaotic, destructive force, but a powerful king whose Upper-Egyptian cults lost ground to the Lower-Egyptian cults of Osiris and Horus.

Seth the Destroyer

Seth's violent, destructive nature was reputed to have been demonstrated from birth. He was said to have torn himself savagely from the womb of his mother, Nut. This is possibly a symbol for the destruction and chaos that can sometimes occur when a new order is being established. Seth became associated with forces of nature and aspects of the ancient world that were feared. He was the god of the desert, the sea, stormy weather and foreign lands.

This latter association with foreign territories is, in part, indicated by Seth's link with the goddesses Astarte and Anat, who were drawn into the Egyptian pantheon from the semitic mythology of Syria and Canaan. During his contest with Horus, Seth is offered these goddesses as consorts, as a consolation for Horus being awarded the kingship of Egypt. Seth was originally linked with his sister, Nephthys, but her role as his consort had ceased after the murder of Osiris. These foreign associations suggest a god whose influence is in exile and who may represent common fears of the unknown or of things beyond Egyptian jurisdiction and control.

The Symbology of Seth

In addition to the hippopotamus, the crocodile and the boar, Seth was associated with many other animals including the panther and a mythical creature called the *hiu*, which was a snake with the head of a donkey. In almost all cases, animals linked to Seth were feared or had some kind of taboo attached to them. The symbology of Seth also included the lettuce, which was said to have been a favourite food of the god!

The link between Seth and the hippopotamus comes from an episode in the contest for the throne of Egypt. Seth challenges Horus to a trial of endurance where they both become hippopotomi competing to stay submerged under water.

SETH IN A READING

Upright

If you have chosen this stone tablet in a reading then it is time to create a new order in your life. Sometimes the creation of new beliefs, new relationships and new patterns of behaviour can seem fraught with confusion and chaos. It may even appear that your whole world is falling apart as the old order of your life comes crashing down around you, and there may be a sense of instability and loss. However, this is not a negative time, but a time of opportunity and new direction. Your divine purpose is emerging and your higher awareness is asserting itself. Once you let go of the fear and trust your ability to handle change, the new phase that is being born will begin to make sense to you; the stormy weather will clear.

Seth has much to teach us about the creative nature of conflict. Many of us do not know how to handle confrontation and we waste energy in hiding from perceived conflict or reacting with aggression and violence. Often, facing our fears calmly and asserting our needs and desires clearly can have a magical effect. Extraordinary compromises can be reached, and even situations that do not contain the potential for compromise offer a multitude of creative solutions beyond what we currently think possible. If we are wrapped up in fear and aggression we lose our objectivity, misdirect our imagination, stifle our intuition and limit our options. On the other hand, when we do our best to calm our fearful or angry thoughts, get as clear as we can be about our true feelings and face a situation head on, then we begin to transform our lives.

The stone of Seth can augur a time when some key relationships in your life are going through dramatic change and growth. Many relationships will be able to ride the storms to become stronger, more loving and more harmonious, while some will not.

Alternatively, the dramatic change you are experiencing could be related to your career, your place of work and the hierarchy around you. While it is good to be committed to the relationships and projects that you have created in your life, it is important to recognize that needs change and the breakdown of any situation, as destructive as it may initially appear to be, can liberate all parties to create something new and better.

Reversed

If the stone tablet is reversed then you are a force for dramatic change in the life of another person. You may not intend to affect or influence others but your actions cannot fail to be transformative and disruptive at this time. You may find that even the simplest act causes a chain reaction affecting not just one but a number of other people.

Remember that in being powerful you can also respect the power and the rights of others. Making sure that your needs are met does not have to be congruent with exploiting others or depriving them of their ability to meet their own needs. Similarly, if you sacrifice yourself to the needs and whims of another person then you need to recognize that it is your choice to do so and that you can make a different choice that will be healthier for you both. Begin a process of change by knowing that when you are true to yourself, honest with others and willing to see all sides of an argument, then everyone really can win.

Attributes

If this stone tablet represents a person then they may well be foreign or alien to you in some way. Their beliefs and behaviour are quite different to your own and you do not immediately understand them. Perhaps it is you who fears being misunderstood. Alternatively, this stone represents someone whose influence you fear. It could be a figure of authority whom you invest with the power to make or break your success, or someone whose presence appears to threaten the established order of your life. Let go of the fear and trust yourself. In western astrology, the qualities of Seth most directly relate to the signs of Aries and Scorpio.

Meditation

Close your eyes, breathe deeply and relax. Focus on any areas of conflict, disagreement or fear you are experiencing at this time or any unresolved conflict from your past. Think about the details of this disruption. How does it affect your life? How do you feel about it? Imagine this drama or conflict as a storm. This could be a rain storm with thunder and lightning or a dust storm of red desert sand. Picture yourself surrounded by a cocoon of bright, white light that shields and protects you as you walk straight through the middle of the storm. As you walk, see how beautiful this disturbance can be when you do not have to fear it, and see yourself arriving on the other side, safe and unharmed. Once the storm has settled, see how new and fresh everything looks.

POSITIVE AFFIRMATIONS

I am safe with my power.
Out of destruction comes creativity and harmony.
It is safe for me to disperse the old and create the new.
I release the past and trust my life to bless me with new gifts.
I am able to harness and handle my divine purpose.
The forces of nature heal and support me.
I am loved and accepted wherever I go.

NEPHTHYS

Goddess of Preservation

— Shadow —

— Guardianship —

— Retreat —

— Grief —

The goddess Nephthys is often described as 'the lady of the mansion' and this is reflected by the hieroglyphic mansion symbol that she bears upon her head within many depictions. She is the sister of Seth, Isis and Osiris, and prior to the murder of Osiris she is also Seth's consort. She is quite mysterious and much less is known about her than her three siblings. Nephthys is a funerary goddess, so she is often concerned with the preservation and protection of the body after death. She embodies the healing power of grief as well as the gentle and perhaps silent guardianship of others. She indicates the wisdom of retreating from life in order to grieve, reflect, receive new insights and recharge depleted energy. Her colours are muted greens and silvery greys.

The Grief of Nephthys

The association between Nephthys and grief comes from her response to the murder of Osiris and her subsequent behaviour. After her husband Seth has mutilated Osiris and scattered the pieces of his body throughout the land, Nephthys sides with her sister Isis and assists her in the search for the dismembered corpse. She and Isis assume the shape of kites and mourn inconsolably for Osiris. The grief of Nephthys is perhaps symbolic of the human grief experienced at the loss of a sibling, a lover or a figure of great power and destiny. For Nephthys, Osiris embodied all three.

The Roles of Nephthys

Because the two goddesses were so closely linked, Nephthys is often thought to be another face of Isis, her clone or her shadow. Certainly, she often seems to take a subordinate role to her sister and does not appear to have had her own cult centre. However, she is an important archetype in her own right and may well have had greater significance than is currently believed. Perhaps an aspect of her obscurity comes from her mysterious nature. She is a hidden goddess who represents the receptive qualities within us all. She is the dark or shadow side of human nature: the unconscious mind, intuition, perceptivity, invisibility and retreat.

Nephthys is an archetype who embodies many roles and human conditions. She is the estranged wife, a woman who chooses to leave her destructive husband and step out on her own to create a new life for herself. She is the mistress and mother: she had a liaison with her brother, Osiris, and had his son, Anubis. Perhaps her greatest role, Nephthys is the archetype of devoted sisterhood. She and Isis seem to bear no jealousy over their love for Osiris, and Nephthys willingly assists and grieves with her sister. Their relationship is based upon sisterly love and trust as well as their mutual loss.

Funerary Rites

As funerary goddesses, Nephthys and Isis were guardians of the tomb. They were often depicted at the head and the foot of a body so they could care for the deceased and protect them on their journey. Alongside Isis, Nephthys provided special protection for the monarch, weeping for him on his death, symbolically mourning him as her lost brother. Like Isis, she is sometimes depicted suckling the king, who was occasionally called the 'menstrual blood' of Nephthys.

The Egyptian fascination with life after death spawned intricate funerary rites. Bodies were mummified and preserved so that they would remain in a good condition for the life to come. As one of the tutelary, or guardian, goddesses charged with watching over the mummified organs of the deceased, Nephthys was also associated with the wrappings of the mummified body which were seen as essential for preservation. However, these wrappings were also feared as a possible encumbrance; the king was challenged to free himself from his bindings or to escape from 'the tresses of Nephthys'.

NEPHTHYS IN A READING

Upright

If you have chosen this stone tablet in a reading then now is a time to retreat from the world to contemplate your next move, come to terms with your feelings and regain the energy that you need to begin a new cycle of life and creativity. Preserving your strength now will benefit you in immeasurable ways in the near and distant future. This time is a gift for anyone who is wishing to develop stamina and pace themselves sensibly as they fulfil their divine purpose or progress steadily towards their life goals.

Perhaps you wish to have some time alone so that you can correct the flow of emotional energy in your life. By acknowledging and expressing your sadness you make yourself available for more joy, and by allowing yourself to grieve you liberate yourself from the past and make yourself available for new experiences, relationships and opportunities. We often underestimate the power of grief and sometimes rush to create something new when an important relationship or project has come to an end. Instead, we need to allow ourselves enough stillness, peace and contemplation for the completion of one phase and the conception of another. Only then can we be sure that each new choice we make is based upon our highest potential and not upon the unfinished business of the past.

The stone of Nephthys augurs a time of shadow, when we are more receptive than normal and need to concentrate on nurturing ourselves rather than rushing around, taking care of others. Nephthys is not a negative or miserable teacher; she is a sweet soul of comfort, peace and strength who can bring much joy if you allow yourself the solitude, stillness and retreat she offers. When we retreat from the world we can heal our wounds, develop our psychic abilities, refuel our creativity and rediscover ourselves.

Nephthys also encourages us to leave behind our competitive impulses and concentrate on building relationships of mutual trust and harmony. There is no space for jealousy now. Linked with this is the gift of sisterhood or brotherhood. You will gain greatly from developing friendships with your peers or from same-sex relationships.

Reversed

If this stone tablet is reversed then you may be the focus for someone else's retreat or grief. Perhaps you are missed by someone who dearly loves you or perhaps your recent absence has created ripples of loss within your family, social circle or working environment. Alternatively, your influence is a nurturing, protective one that enables someone you care for to retreat from the world and enjoy a period of relative calm. Your influence preserves the good qualities of a situation or relationship while allowing anything outworn to disintegrate and die. When moving house, leaving a job, finishing a period of study or coming to the end of a project, it is important to have some quiet time to put our affairs in order before moving on. Your presence makes it easier for others to sift the wheat from the chaff and discard anything that no longer supports their life path. Your love and commitment helps to dispel any physical, mental or emotional factors that may otherwise inhibit their future potential.

Attributes

If this stone tablet represents a person then they will have great power and dedication concealed by a silent exterior. This is a private person who is not immediately available for scrutiny or intimacy but who is always loving, sweet natured, kind and honourable. They could be a good friend, a devoted parent or sibling, a healer or a psychic. Their skills lie in receptivity, compassion and intuition rather than in active demonstrations of creativity and intent. This person is not motivated by jealousy or given to outbursts of passion, but she or he is quietly seductive and eternally fascinating. The qualities of Nephthys most directly relate to the sign of Capricorn in western astrology.

Meditation

Close your eyes, breathe deeply and relax. Ask for the protection of Nephthys and visualize yourself surrounded by a beautiful web of silver and green threads of light. Within the web you have plenty of space to move freely and breathe but know that you are protected from the outside world. Relax, explore your feelings and recharge your batteries. If you are completing something – a relationship, an experience or a project – review your thoughts and feelings about it. Take time to bless what you are leaving behind, honour yourself for moving through this period of your life and allow yourself to grieve if you need to. To complete the meditation, imagine emerging from these threads of light like a butterfly from a cocoon. You are refreshed, renewed and ready to move on to new and better experiences.

POSITIVE AFFIRMATIONS

I find beauty and support within stillness.
My life is filled with sweet sisterhood (brotherhood).
I make friends with the shadow side of my personality.
I am blessed with the sweetness of joy and sadness.
I withdraw to recharge myself and re-emerge to shine.
I am receptive to new avenues of expression.
I am intuitive, compassionate, wise and strong.

HORUS

Lord of the Skies

— Vision —

— Majesty —

— Communication —

— Balance —

The god Horus is the son of Osiris and Isis. He is a visionary energy: the lord of prophecy, music, art, humour and beauty. One of the most prominent of ancient-Egyptian gods, Horus was originally the god of the hunting people and was symbolized by a falcon. Later, he became identified with the sun and was the symbol of majesty, archetype of the Pharaohs. Horus, the divine falcon, became the sky god with the sun as his right eye and the moon as his left. His is the all-seeing eye of clairvoyant ability, heightened vision and expanded awareness. The four elements were at his command: earth, wind, fire and water. Horus represents the balance of the natural world and is also linked to the eastern horizon and foreign lands. He is identified with the colour yellow.

The Conception of Horus

Following the murder of Osiris by Seth, the goddesses Isis and Nephthys roamed the land in search of the dismembered pieces of Osiris's body, which Seth had scattered to a number of sites throughout Egypt. On reassembling the body of Osiris, Isis is able to use her magic to resurrect him momentarily so that they may copulate and conceive a son. Thus, Horus, the avenging heir of Osiris and rightful successor to the throne of Egypt, is conceived.

Many stories focus on Horus as a child born in secret at Khemmis and hidden in the papyrus marshes. Isis, with all of her magic and guile, conceals and protects him until he is old enough to challenge his uncle, Seth, for the throne.

Horus and Divine Kingship

The dispute for sovereignty between Horus and Seth is a long, complex affair that reflects the importance of both gods in the mythology and culture of ancient Egypt. The sun god Re is often said to have been the judge who presided over the tribunal, initially dividing the territory between them. Seth is offered the kingship of Upper Egypt and Horus the kingship of Lower Egypt. However, some accounts of this dispute tell of Re changing his mind and not favouring Horus at all.

An eighty-year contest then ensues between Horus and Seth as they both attempt to prove themselves to the court and outwit each other. On many occasions it is the magic of Isis that once again protects Horus. With her help, Horus even thwarts an incident of sexual assault by his uncle and shames him in the process.

Horus, in his successful bid as rightful heir to the throne of a united Egypt, became representative of the Pharaoh's divine right to kingship, and is one of the gods whose influence conveys sovereignty and power.

The Eye of Horus

At one point in the dispute between Horus and Seth, Seth pursues his nephew into the desert and cuts out his eyes. Horus is discovered by Hathor who is sometimes described as his mother, rather than Isis. It is she who restores his eyes using gazelle's milk. The lunar eye of Horus or *udjat* subsequently became a powerful image that symbolized kingship, strength, purification and protection.

For the Egyptians, the *udjat* was a totem of protection that was frequently worn on a necklace, placed in the wrappings of mummified bodies and, in some cases, painted onto coffins. Later, the Greeks, who were strongly influenced by Egyptian culture, painted a similar eye symbol on the prow of their boats to bring good fortune and protection to their craft.

Today, the Eye of Horus still has a powerful influence. Its likeness turns up again and again in popular jewellery, art and design. Many people are drawn to it without knowing of its significance, perhaps subtly awakened to their own innate connection to the ancient Egyptians and the Osirans.

HORUS IN A READING

Upright

If you have chosen this stone tablet in a reading then it is a time for receiving messages from the world around you and from your world within. Perhaps the beauty and the wildness of the natural world is telling you to awaken to your natural talents. How could you express your unique creativity today and uncover your wild, untamed spirit? Perhaps you feel your inner vision stirring with prophecies of things to come, either for yourself or for someone else. Look for all the messages that come your way today; some may come to you via a letter or a telephone call, others could arrive as pictures glimpsed by your inner eye.

The stone of Horus augurs a time of balance and invites you to become aware of any area of your life that needs to be balanced in some way. Are you spending too much time working and not leaving enough time for yourself to sing, dance and create joy? Remember that recreation time is not wasted time. It is the time when you literally re-create yourself anew, your vision, your enthusiasm, your direction and your sense of wonder. Perhaps your relationships need to be balanced in some way too, so you are giving and receiving love in equal quantity.

In finding balance, Horus reminds us of the value of protection. Do you need to protect your creativity, speak up for your vision or honour your insights? Do you need to stand up for what is rightfully yours and take your place as the sovereign of your destiny? When combined with vision and clear communication, the qualities of honesty and integrity will often provide you with the best protection. In addition, acknowledge your fears and do your best to nurture a belief that you are always safe wherever you go. In your mind you could visualize an eye of Horus at your forehead, another at your heart, a third at your feet and a fourth on your back. Imagine these protective eyes extending their influence to keep every part of you safe and protected always.

Reversed

If this stone tablet is reversed then you are the bringer of messages for another person. Perhaps you are being invited to write a letter, make a telephone call or pass on information that will encourage someone to expand their personal vision and awareness, bringing a healing solution. How does your personal vision inspire others into action? It is a gift to be a visionary for your family, your friends and your colleagues, providing the world with positivity and insight. However, ensure that you maintain a balance between inspiring others to act and acting on their behalf. Make sure that your vision does not rob others of their ability to think and act for themselves.

Alternatively, you may provide a protective influence for another person, endorsing their right to be who they are and helping them to follow their chosen path or profession. Be a guide, offer your support and protection for as long as your influence helps others to grow, but if they need to spread their wings like a falcon and take to the skies then you need to be willing to let go.

Attributes

If this stone tablet represents a person in your life then they will be someone whose influence encourages you to ease up and see the bigger picture of your life. They are visionary and inspirational and they easily inspire others. This person may well be communicative, extrovert, bright, humorous and fun; willing to shine these qualities in your direction. This is someone who remains youthful, beautiful and charismatic, whatever their years. They are often the centre of attention, whether they wish to be or not. Despite their youthful and visionary attributes, they may also be a little innocent or naive at times. The qualities of Horus most directly relate to the signs of Gemini and Leo in western astrology.

Meditation

Close your eyes, breathe deeply and relax. Focus your attention on the centre of your forehead, the area that is often known as the third eye. In your mind, imagine that you have a physical eye there and picture yourself opening that eye.

See this third eye as beautiful, brightly coloured and shining. It is able to see with love, wisdom, compassion and inspiration. Imagine yourself 'seeing' any information that would aid you with your healing, personal development or spiritual growth at this time. You may imagine symbols, shapes, colours or cinematic images.

It does not matter if you do not see or imagine anything when you first do this. The visualization of this eye will help to expand your inner vision and awaken your intuition. Complete the meditation by picturing the eye closing again, to keep your vision safe and protected. If you received any insights then write them down and act upon them.

POSITIVE AFFIRMATIONS

I trust my inner vision.
I am balanced and harmonious.
I expand my creativity.
I communicate my power and my unique insights.
I claim the joy and success that is rightfully mine.
I am always safe and protected.
I expand my awareness.

BASTET

Cat Goddess

— Perfume —

— Purity —

— Peacefulness —

— Affection —

The goddess Bastet is usually depicted as the beloved cat of Egypt; an animal that was sacred to the Egyptians. However, earlier versions of her indicate that she was originally a lioness with a vicious, vengeful nature. Often she is represented as a woman with a cat's head and sometimes she is displayed with a litter of kittens. The hieroglyph of her name is the symbol for a sealed alabaster perfume jar. Perfume would have been an important part of the ritual purity involved in her cult. In some traditions Bastet was thought to be the daughter of Isis and Osiris and the sister of Horus. The most prominent centre of her cult was at Bubastis in the north-east delta. Her colour is turquoise.

War and Peace

The cat goddess Bastet evolved from aggressive origins, depicted as a warrior lioness. She is often linked with the lioness Sakhmet, a powerful and savage goddess who was said to breathe fire against the enemies of the Pharaoh. Legends tell of Bastet, in the form of a lioness, spending a period of time in exile before returning to Egypt as a placid, sweet-natured cat. However, like all cats, she retained the aggressive impulses of the predator. She is sometimes depicted as a daughter of the sun god Re, decapitating Apophis, the underworld snake.

Bastet's transformation from warrior into peacemaker could have reflected a political change in ancient Egypt or could simply be indicative of the spread of the domestic cat during later dynasties. Whatever social or cultural developments influenced her worship and symbology, Bastet is an archetype who effectively epitomizes the taming of the savage, bestial forces within human nature. She is the embodiment of civilization and the triumph of diplomacy over conflict.

Perfume and Purity

Bastet's cult included rituals of perfume and purity. It is possible that she was linked to the cycles of menstruation and fertility. The cleansing and purification involved in her worship may have represented the body cleansing itself during its monthly cycle. In addition, the cat was a symbol of sexual availability. The perfume of Bastet could have been the scent of seduction.

Bastet was also a goddess of music and dance. Like Hathor, the cow goddess, Bastet was associated with the sistrum, a musical instrument that was a kind of rattle. When the sistrum was played in the celebration of these goddesses, there was often the effigy of a cat (for Bastet) or a cow (for Hathor) carved upon the top. Both Bastet and Hathor were goddesses linked to sensuality, sexuality and feminine power. Bastet was a goddess of northern Egypt while Hathor's worship was stronger in the south.

The Cult of the Cat

The cat was honoured with respect and great affection by the ancient Egyptians. The 'great cat of Heliopolis' referred to in the *Book of the Dead*, probably a jungle cat indigenous to the Nile delta, was honoured because of its hostility to snakes. Cats were celebrated with ritual burial which involved being mummified, dressed with elaborate wrappings and given faces of humour or character. There were large cemeteries of mummified cats at Bubastis and other areas where the worship of Bastet was prominent.

Throughout history the cat has engendered powerful feelings of affection or repulsion. It is an animal that is often linked with magical practices, spiritual awareness and potent sexuality. Perhaps it is not surprising that European Christian extremists in the Middle Ages associated the cat with devil worship. For the Egyptians, however, there is no evidence to suggest that cats were seen as anything other than a positive influence in their lives.

BASTET IN A READING

Upright

If you have chosen this stone tablet in a reading then it is time to make peace with yourself and seek harmony within all of your relationships. If someone is taking you for granted or trespassing upon your territory then it is important that you stand up for your rights and clearly state your needs. However, remember that the key to success is assertion, not aggression. Communicate as clearly and as honestly as possible without either demanding that you get your own way or apologizing for yourself. You will be surprised at how easy it is to negotiate. A peaceful attitude combined with strength of purpose brings determination and creative solutions. The stone of Bastet may augur a time when you need to claim your own personal space. When you honour your need to be alone then the time you spend with lovers, family and friends becomes more peaceful, more harmonious and, ultimately, more pleasurable.

Bastet is a goddess of purity whose influence encourages us to cleanse ourselves of anything that no longer supports us in health and happiness. What relationships have you outgrown? What habits no longer serve you? Do you need to let go of old, negative expectations or patterns of belief? Could you simplify or balance your diet so your body can safely eliminate toxins and regain its natural rhythms? Safe and gentle purification now will bring you numerous benefits in the near and distant future.

Bastet also speaks of perfume and ritual. If the pace of life is unsettling then it is important to take time for the simple things that stabilize you. You may benefit from regular meditations or cat naps, a daily walk or a few minutes to yourself, morning and evening, to be alone with your thoughts. Pampering is ideal: have a massage, go for regular sessions with a healer or a therapist and, in particular, have long baths with fragrant essential oils. Your sense of smell is especially important now so keep your environment clean and fresh. A change of air will change your mood.

Reversed

If this stone tablet is reversed then your influence could encourage others to clean up their act. Your love and affection creates a safe space for them to drop negative or destructive habits in favour of positive ones that will support them in health and harmony. You do not need to preach your philosophy or nag other people to make changes; quite the opposite. Your positive example is the most powerful catalyst for change. Just love and accept other people, stay committed to your own well-being, and those around you will want to make positive changes too.

The fragrance of your personality charms others and you are able to exert influence through guile as well as through direct communication. Perhaps because you are quite self-contained at this time and are not actively seeking the attention or approval of others, you discover affection, opportunity and success in abundance. You can afford to be selective. If someone is offering you something that you do not really want, then acknowledge them for their gift but know that you can refuse. Saying 'no' with good grace allows you to say 'yes' with enthusiasm when the timing and the offer is right.

Attributes

If this stone tablet represents a person then they will be affectionate and caring but also quite aloof. They are self-contained, probably attractive and compelling. Their charisma comes from a natural, understated beauty rather than a glamorous exterior. They can be powerfully seductive and very sweet natured; their influence is subtle but their impact is profound. Despite their guile, they often have clear boundaries and their communication can be precise and direct. These qualities most directly relate to the signs of Virgo and Libra in western astrology.

Meditation

Close your eyes, breathe deeply and relax. Visualize yourself undressing and stepping into a warm bath imbued with magical fragrant oils that relax you, bringing you feelings of peace and well-being. With each breath you take, the sweet fragrances heal you and transform your mood, taking you to a place of increased awareness and heightened sensuality. Imagine also, that the essences cleanse you of any toxins, fears, disease or disharmony. All your negative thoughts and beliefs dissolve away into the fragrant waters. When you are ready, see yourself stepping out of the bath and picture the water flowing away, safely taking all negativity and disharmony with it. Visualize yourself anointing your body with more fragrant oils that enhance your natural beauty whilst also giving you an aura of strength, self-respect and protection. Complete this visualization by seeing yourself dress in a beautiful new set of clothes.

POSITIVE AFFIRMATIONS

I make peace with myself.
I have purity of purpose and clarity of direction.
I easily recognize my own beauty.
I am at peace with the world.
My territory is sacred, my space is honoured and respected.
I am guided by my higher nature.
I have clear boundaries.

ANUBIS

Lord of the Afterlife

— Healing —

— Guidance —

— Lightness of Spirit —

— Protection —

Anubis is generally depicted as a crouching dog or jackal, although he also appears as a dog-headed or jackal-headed man. His coat is black, the colour of death and fertility. In some accounts he is said to be the son of the goddess Nephthys who conceived him during a liaison with Osiris, the husband of her sister, Isis. Isis is then said to have adopted Anubis as her own son. The special healing powers of Anubis cast him as the rescuer, working with unconscious or anaesthetized people and leading the blind. He protects all who cannot see, whether through physical impairment, innocence or lack of worldly knowledge. In this way he provides safety and guidance for travellers and brings healing to those who are suffering. His colour is terracotta.

Anubis the Guardian

Anubis was the guardian of the dead and of embalming. He protected mummified bodies from evil forces and was able to provide guidance for the soul. The bodies of kings were embalmed in the name of Anubis and in some ceremonies a high priest would wear a jackal mask and act as the representative of the god. Anubis was thought to purify the body with unguents and anoint it with oils before wrapping it in linen and watching over the burial chamber. His image appears on the walls of tombs and is painted on coffins.

Although he is associated with death and dying, Anubis is, on the whole, a benign figure. The Egyptian belief in an afterlife gave great comfort to those contemplating their own physical mortality, as well as to the friends and family members of the recently deceased as they came to terms with their loss. In life, Anubis assists us in our search for our inner selves and he brings the two worlds of the conscious and unconscious together. His influence is compassionate, patient, stable, trustworthy and strong. This magical god is also a divine clown who brings humour to shatter any heaviness around the heart and to turn seriousness into the healing sound of laughter.

The Hall of Judgement

Anubis was thought to have very special healing gifts. He was responsible for leading the spirit into the Hall of Judgement and for weighing the heart of the deceased in the presence of Osiris and a company of forty-two gods. He was imagined to claim the heart and adjust the scales to bring an accurate account of its integrity. He would then free the dead king from mortal restrictions so that he may take his place amongst the gods. The owner of an honest heart is guided by Anubis to his rightful position at the throne of Osiris.

The belief in the immortality of a dying king may well have helped maintain a level of political stability just prior to and immediately after the Pharaoh's death. Placing trust in a guide and protector to take care of the dead on their journey may have created a sense of grace, peace and stability.

Desert Dogs

In many cultures the dog is viewed as a beast of loyalty, guardianship and protection. Dogs are traditionally pack animals with a strong sense of their role within the family group. They are relatively easy to domesticate and their pack loyalty is readily transferred to a human family. In this way they are not unlike pre-industrial human beings who depended upon a clan or community for survival and for whom a level of personal loyalty must have been essential.

The figure of Anubis was probably based upon the scavenging desert jackal. He was thought to provide leadership for the many souls buried in the cemeteries on the west bank of the Nile. What better guardian to watch over the graveyards of Egypt than a divine jackal who could repel the unwanted attentions of mortal desert dogs?

ANUBIS IN A READING

Upright

If you have chosen this stone tablet in a reading then you are being guided into the depths of your psyche and urged to trust your intuition. Solutions may come to you through dream images as you sleep or through symbols that linger in your waking mind. Insights could come during meditation, shattering your personal illusions and liberating you from negative expectations, extreme seriousness or self-delusion. Anubis offers you safety as you experience the death of some aspect of your life that you have outgrown. Perhaps it is time to release all self-imposed limitations and see yourself as the expansive, powerful person that you truly are, with an infinite ability to heal yourself and transform your life.

Anubis always augurs healing. Picking this stone can indicate the success of medical or complementary treatments and encourages you to seek help and guidance for anything that is troubling you. It also indicates that the power to heal yourself is within your grasp; particularly if you are willing to look at where disharmony, stress or tension may be self-imposed and make appropriate changes in lifestyle or attitude.

The protection of Anubis is important if you are contemplating surgery or some other radical medical procedure, especially anything involving anaesthetics. First, ask for the guidance of Anubis to help you to explore other options. Is this surgery necessary for your health or would another approach be more beneficial? Do as much research as you can and do not be afraid to ask questions of doctors, health workers and complementary therapists. If you decide that surgery is the right option for you then, in your thoughts, ask Anubis to guide you safely out of your body while you are under anaesthetic and then to guide you safely back into your body once the procedure is complete. Picture Anubis protecting you, mind, body and soul, as you undergo every stage of your treatment.

Reversed

If this stone tablet is reversed then you may be visiting the dreams of another person to provide healing, reassurance or support deep within their soul. Consciously or unconsciously you could be assisting them with their healing process by guiding them towards their path of power and their ability to heal themselves. It could also be that you are helping someone to complete a relationship so that they can move on to better things. Remember that in letting go of all that is outworn, you, and they, are invoking lightness, liberation and new life.

Alternatively, you may be in a process of training. Now is the perfect time to learn new skills that will aid the healing or evolution of humanity. You could be drawn to train in medicine, counselling, herbalism, spiritual healing, or one of a multitude of healing arts and skills. Your training need not be formal: life may be honing your healing potential through seemingly chance encounters with like-minded souls; experiences that stretch you or challenge you to awaken your innate healing gifts, and information via books, audio tapes or your own inner voices. Certainly your intuitive or psychic skills are growing at this time and they too are given to you for healing.

Attributes

If this stone tablet represents a person then it is someone who offers you compassionate good humour, reassurance and fun. This person has hidden depths. Their lightness of spirit masks great strength and clarity of purpose. He or she may be psychic, otherworldly, mysterious and transformative, and they may offer you acceptance or a listening ear. They could have a youthful appearance but they are an old soul with accumulated wisdom and acute awareness. The qualities of Anubis are most strongly linked to the sign of Pisces in western astrology.

Meditation

Close your eyes, breathe deeply and relax. In your mind's eye, imagine a bright, healing light shining into your heart to bring you reassurance, love, acceptance and peace. The light is golden and beautiful. It melts away all tension from your heart and your chest. Imagine all heaviness, sadness, pain, restriction and seriousness releasing from you, leaving you light-hearted and joyful.

See your heart developing its own radiance as if it has an inner flame that is being rekindled. Allow the light from within and around your heart to spread to every part of you. Picture yourself filling with brilliance and wonder; your body, mind, emotions and spirit healed by your radiant heart. Particularly imagine this light spreading to your feet and your eyes so that your path forward is illuminated with love. Now you are able to see with greater clarity as you step into the unknown adventures ahead of you in your life.

POSITIVE AFFIRMATIONS

My heart is light and free.
I have the perfect health care for my needs.
I am always guided to safety.
My life is filled with laughter and infinite wisdom.
I release my illusions and deepen my understanding.
I have the power to heal myself.
I listen to my intuition.

HATHOR

Mother of the Pharaoh

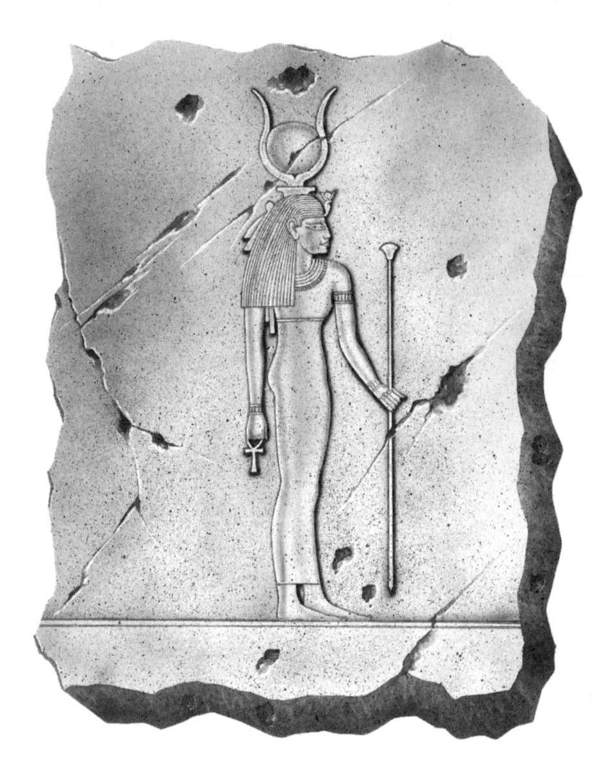

— Destiny —

— Love —

— Birthright —

— Music —

The goddess Hathor is a universal cow goddess who is associated with childbirth. It is said that her womb protected the hawk god Horus and indeed her name literally means 'mansion of Horus'. She is often depicted as a woman who bears a wig, a crown of cow horns and a sun disc on her head. She is also shown as a 'great wild cow' or as a pillar with a human face, a wig and the ears of a cow. Like Isis, she is sometimes described as the mother of the Pharaoh and is therefore associated with birthright and the right to rule. Hathor is a sensual goddess of love, music and beauty. The Greeks associated her with Aphrodite, their goddess of love. Hathor's colours are deep oranges, pinks and peaches: the colours of vitality.

Hathor the Mother

In ancient Egypt, the cow was a positive symbol of feminine power and maternal strength; a perspective that is quite unlike the contemporary view of this animal in the western world. The cow symbology of Hathor displays the predominantly benign nature of this goddess; she is a figure of sensuality, nourishment and motherhood. In some stories she, rather than Isis, is the mother of Horus and it is possible that her connection to Horus pre-dates the Osiran myth where Isis is a central figure. Hathor is also a sky goddess and in this capacity is said to protect the hawk god Horus within her womb. She is the dwelling place, domain or 'mansion' of Horus.

It is because of her maternal connection to Horus that Hathor is often described as the mother of the Pharaoh. Like Isis and other gods and goddesses of the Egyptian pantheon, she was associated with the birthright and destiny of the Egyptian ruler. She is often depicted in the form of a cow suckling the Pharaoh from her udder.

Goddess of Love and Music

Hathor is a sexual goddess who is linked with romantic love, the pleasures of life and the sensual arts. She is associated with music, song and dance, and many erotic dances were dedicated to her; her musical instrument was the sistrum. Hathor's influence is both celebratory and seductive. She is linked to make-up, jewellery, adornment and sensual culinary skills.

Hathor also had a warrior nature which was usually displayed in defence of someone whom she nurtured and loved. Like Bastet, she was sometimes linked to the fire-breathing leonine goddess, Sakhmet, and was, on occasion, depicted as a lioness rather than a cow. She is resourceful in defending Horus during his contest with Seth; although in these stories she uses guile and sexuality rather than her warlike streak. At one point Hathor diffuses a difficult situation by lifting up her dress and exposing herself to her father, Re, who was presiding over the tribunal. In doing so she causes him to laugh, dispelling his black mood so that the proceedings can continue.

Hathor, 'mistress of the southern sycamore' (a reference to her ancient tree cult) is also a funerary goddess. In this capacity she offers safe passage to anyone travelling through the underworld. She provides them with the protection of her outer garment, the *tjesten*. The papyrus was sacred to Hathor and her main cult centre was located at Dendera *(see map on page 8)*.

The Seven Hathors

The seven Hathors were figures not unlike the good fairies of European folklore. Their role was to define the fate of an individual at birth, determining the life path or spiritual lessons that lay ahead. Like Hathor herself, they were depicted as cows and their images appear in tombs and within the *Book of the Dead*. They announce the arrival of great souls and provide an angelic influence in guiding the destiny of us all.

HATHOR IN A READING

Upright

If you have chosen this stone tablet in a reading then this is a time to sing, dance and celebrate life. How can you relax and play a little more, enjoying the sensuality of your body and the ecstasy of your true self? The world is full of beauty that can inspire us all to heal ourselves if we allow it to and can help us to contact our passion and joy. When we look for the beauty within everything, we transcend the ordinary and contact the divine. Often we hold back, scared of letting go to our impulses, but with Hathor's guidance we can allow ourselves to be touched by sensuality and celebration, letting our lives be transformed for the better.

The stone of Hathor augurs a time of restoration. Feelings, experiences or relationships that you thought were lost or that you had forgotten about, now re-emerge. If you thought that joy had faded from your life or that happiness had passed you by then think again. An abundance of wonderful feelings are available to you now if you stay positive and remain open to receive the gifts that life has to offer. If you thought that you would not love again then now is the time to see with new eyes and recognize that love is still available. It is up to you to change your view of the world and be willing to open your heart; the potential to give and receive love is stronger than ever.

Hathor could also be reminding you that your destiny is catching up with you. Positive changes are taking place as the tempo of your life speeds up or slows down. So often we have learned to fear change and expect the worst from new experiences, when the reality available to us is quite different. The music of life is calling you to dance. Be creative, be sensual, expect the best and allow yourself the joy of being alive. Your destiny is glorious!

Reversed

If this stone tablet is reversed then you could be the object of someone else's desire. The light of your beauty shines out from within you to touch the hearts of those around you. Certainly your influence is inspirational and healing as you encourage others by your example to live life to the full and savour the pleasures of each new moment. Perhaps your creativity provides an impulse for others to remember their true feelings, awaken their passions and become realigned with their destiny.

Alternatively, choosing Hathor reversed gives you the message that the only way forward at this time is through love. If you are feeling angry, hurt or scared and your first reaction is to withdraw from other people, then take a big breath and do the reverse, move closer and be as loving to yourself and others as you can. Be honest about all of your feelings; declare and demonstrate your loving intentions.

It is especially important at this time to tell your family that you love them, tell your friends and, of course, if you are in an ongoing romantic relationship, tell your lover or life partner. Most of all, it is important to tell yourself how lovable and special you are. It is easier for us to share our love with others when we have learned to love, care for and cherish ourselves.

Attributes

If this stone tablet represents a person who has come into your life then it will be someone whose care and compassion inspires you to lighten up and get on with the process of living. There is fun to be had and this person knows how to find it. They also have a talent for encouraging others to create fun and frivolity too. This could be someone who loves dressing up and painting the town red or someone who enjoys the sensuality of the natural world, particularly the colours, sounds and smells of the forest. They are often loved and appreciated by other people. In western astrology the qualities of Hathor most directly relate to the sign of Taurus.

Meditation

Close your eyes, breathe deeply and relax. Visualize yourself looking into a full-length mirror and see the image of your body facing you. Picture a deep orange light emanating from your stomach and spreading out to fill and surround every part of you. The light makes you magnetic to joyful, loving experiences and boosts your physical vitality, stimulating your passionate nature. Notice your mirror image beginning to move and dance in front of your eyes; your body is free, flexible, sensual and vibrantly healthy. Any disease or disharmony is safely dispersed by the movement, and the affected area is instantly restored by the light.

As your image dances, see the light around you moving in spirals that spin outwards from your body. You are radiating an inexhaustible supply of positive energy that keeps you protected and makes you magnetic to people, places and situations that reflect your highest growth and potential.

POSITIVE AFFIRMATIONS

I explore my sexuality with joy and pleasure.

I sing, dance and celebrate life.

I awaken the sensual power of my body.

My life is full of opportunities to give and receive love.

I move towards my destiny and my greatest joy.

My passion for living is constantly renewed.

I nurture my joyful nature.

AMUN

Lord of Concealment

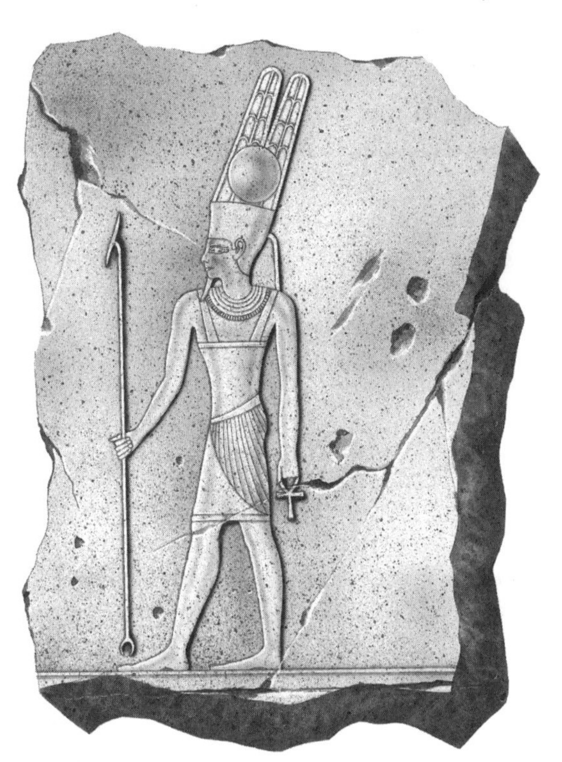

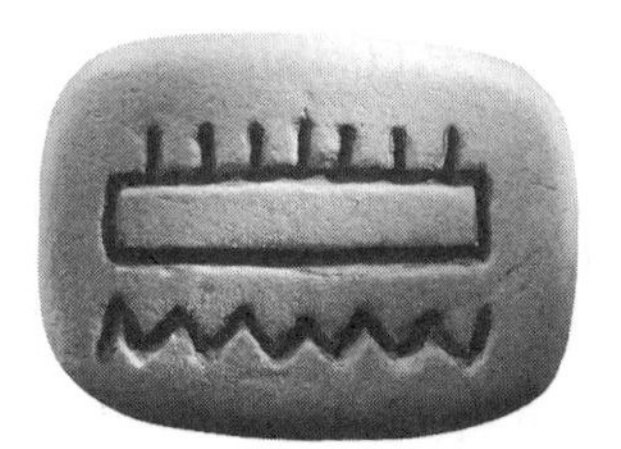

— Invisibility —

— Supremacy —

— Manifestation —

— Strength —

The god Amun is supreme in the Egyptian pantheon; his influence began in primeval times and extended into the New Kingdom when his divinity was enhanced by being reinterpreted as a mysterious manifestation of the ancient sun god Re. He is sometimes depicted on a throne like a Pharaoh and wearing a crown of high plumes. At Thebes he was thought to be the forerunner of all other gods and goddesses. Amun was believed to be invisible to mortals; the name of 'Amun' translates to mean concealment or 'the hidden one'. The hieroglyph of his name is written phonetically and includes the symbols for a gaming board (Mn) and water (N). Amun's flesh is the blue of lapis lazuli, a highly prized stone worthy of a god.

The Origins of Amun

A god of Thebes, Amun may have been a local deity or he could have been an adopted foreign god. Certainly his worship spread and in the New Kingdom he became the supreme god of the Egyptian pantheon. In Heliopolis, he was seen as the mysterious face of the sun god Re. The two gods were combined under the name of Amun-Re.

The Thebans believed Amun to be self-created. He was thought to have mysteriously brought himself into existence before the formation of matter and the advent of any other deities. He was the spark of creation from which all other divine entities and all life sprang. In some ways he corresponds to the universal father god of Judaism and Christianity, and his origins may have been geographically similar. However, his facelessness and mysterious nature are also reminiscent of the great mystery that is central to the beliefs of many first nation people of the Americas. In short, he is a god who embodies many universal truths and represents the intangible forces of creation.

Amun the Magician

Amun, although concealed or invisible to the gaze of mortals, is associated with eyesight and was called on to bring healing to the eyes. Spells in the name of Amun were used to prevent eye injuries and cure a number of ailments. He was a magician who could be invoked to cure scorpion bites, provide protection from crocodiles and snakes and preserve the bodies of the dead.

God of the People

Amun was thought to be a god who advocated the rights and needs of the ordinary Egyptian. He was said to uphold the principles of justice and protect the rights of the poor in the law courts. He was seen as a compassionate deity, beyond bribery and against corruption of any kind. His compassion extended to workmen and travellers seeking protection on long journeys. Although a god of the common man, Amun was also a god of royalty. He was often considered to be the father of the king. From the Middle Kingdom onwards some of the Pharaohs were given or assumed names that incorporated the name of the god. An example is Tutankhamun (Tut-Ankh-Amun).

In Thebes, Amun was the prominent god of a divine triad. The grouping of divine patriarch, divine matriarch and divine child was a popular one at a number of cult centres throughout the ancient-Egyptian world *(see pages 9–10)*. The Theban triad of Amun, his consort, Mut, and their adopted child, Khonsu, had a particularly powerful cult following. Little is known about Mut. Her name translated means 'Mother' and she may well have embodied the divine maternal qualities that other, more prominent goddesses also represented. It is possible that most of the information about her was lost or destroyed, but it is also possible that she reflected the mysterious nature of her more famous husband. Like Sakhmet in the north, she was sometimes depicted with the head of a lion; her other form was as a woman with a vulture headdress.

AMUN IN A READING

Upright

If you have chosen this stone tablet in a reading then be prepared for mysterious forces to blow through your life. Things are changing around you that appear to be beyond your comprehension and beyond your control. If you attempt to fight those changes or force your will upon them then you will only place limitations on the opportunities and gifts that are coming your way. Trust yourself, trust life and surrender to the flow of the universe. There is a bigger picture to the events that are unfolding, but it is not available for you to see at this moment.

The stone of Amun often augurs a time when your impact is greater from a distance and by reputation than from immediate, personal contact. In business, it would be better to be directing proceedings from behind the scenes, delegating to colleagues or junior employees rather than being hands on with every task. This could well be a time for promotion, moving up the ranks or gaining in personal power. To be sure of success, pause and consider your approach before you apply yourself. With family and friends, too, you may appear to be gaining a new sovereignty, becoming more sure of yourself, maturing in attitude and gaining more respect. However, it is important not to dissipate this new position by trying too hard to be all things to all people. It is better to retreat and consolidate your energy. Much can be achieved personally and professionally when wisdom and restraint are applied.

Spiritually you are growing in strength and awareness. It no longer serves you to have a narrow view of yourself and a limited view of your abilities. Your growth and evolution may not always seem tangible or visible but you are developing nonetheless. You have the potential to create the harmony, fulfilment and happiness that you desire in your life. Honour your dreams and allow the mystery of the universe to guide you onwards and upwards.

Reversed

If this stone tablet is reversed then you may find yourself defending the rights of other people. You might be seeking justice for someone who is unable to speak up for themselves or putting the needs of the family or community ahead of your own individual desires and ambitions. You are in an ideal position to create opportunities for others, stimulating their personal development, strengthening their self-esteem and perhaps even advancing their career. You may soon discover that helping other people to win provides you with the best formula for your own success.

At present, you may need to operate behind the scenes or be a mysterious benefactor, but in the long term, your service of other people will not go unrewarded. Perhaps it is best to think of yourself as a guardian angel and trust that no gift of angelic grace is ever lost or ever goes unnoticed. If you become the guardian angel today then someone else will act as your guardian angel tomorrow. There is equal joy in giving and receiving; it is important to make the most of both and remember that your influence brings magical and mysterious changes for all concerned.

Attributes

If this stone tablet represents a person who has come into your life then they will have a powerful impact upon you. They may become intimately involved in your life and instrumental in your destiny whilst remaining enigmatic and mysterious. He or she will probably know much more about you than you are ever likely to know about them. Sometimes this stone can represent more than one person. It could be a committee or a collection of authoritative figures whose decisions affect the course of your life: usually for the better. In western astrology the qualities of Amun most directly relate to the signs of Aries and Sagittarius.

Meditation

Close your eyes, breathe deeply and relax. In your mind's eye picture yourself putting on a cloak of invisibility. The fabric feels soft on your skin and is warm, protective and magical. Visualize yourself putting it over your head and allowing the folds of cloth to fall to your feet, covering your whole body. Imagine yourself becoming invisible as you put your arms into the sleeves and pull up the hood.

The cloak of invisibility makes you magnetic to positive, loving attention, harmonious relationships, positive experiences and a sense of well-being. It keeps you safely removed from all negative or unwanted attention and helps you to deflect the experiences that do not serve your highest healing potential. Picture yourself walking into a room full of people and only being visible to those whose intentions are honourable. Within your cloak of invisibility you grow in strength, balance and happiness.

POSITIVE AFFIRMATIONS

I surrender to the divine.
My life develops in new and unexpected ways.
I am willing to let go and trust the process of life.
I enjoy the mystery of each new moment.
I am blessed with infinite opportunities.
I support the growth and development of other people.
I am an angel for myself and others.

RE

God of the Sun

— Journeying —
— Cycles —
— Illumination —
— Creation —

Re is the sun god of Heliopolis whose other forms include Atum and Khepri. Most commonly, Re is depicted as a falcon wearing the fiery disk of the sun on his head. When he is shown passing through the underworld he takes the form of a ram-headed god or an old man. The sun crossing the sky was thought to be the body of the sun god, or sometimes it was considered to be his eye. As the combined god Atum-Re, he is a creator god who is endowed with many life-giving properties; sometimes called 'the weeper', he is said to have created humankind from his tears. He also ordered the cycle of the three seasons that make up the Egyptian year. The colour associated with Re is the gold of the sun.

The Orbit of the Sun

Re is the sun god of Heliopolis, city of the sun. His cult centre was within an area of the city called Yunu. The name of the god was also the name that the Egyptians gave to the solar orb.

Within Egyptian history, many significant gods were combined or became associated with one another. This was partly to do with the rise and fall of various cult centres and the subsequent rationalization of popular mythology. As a powerful deity, Re became associated with many other gods. Most significantly he was thought to be a later incarnation of the creator god Atum, great grandfather of Isis and Osiris. The scarab-beetle god, Khepri, was considered to be the face of the sun god in the morning, the solar disk of Re was his form at midday and the ram's head of Atum or Khnum was his evening visage. His other powerful association was with Amun, principal god of Thebes. As Amun-Re they combined to become one of the foremost deities of the ancient-Egyptian world.

A later view of the sun's cycle imagined Re as a child in the morning, born of a lotus blossom, then towards the middle of the day as a monkey shooting rays of light, and finally as an old man in the evening.

Re the Creator

Re's associations with both Atum and Amun emphasized his role as a creator god. He was thought to have emerged from the primeval waters at the beginning of time, standing upon a sacred mound called the *Benben*. The Egyptians imagined Re to have created humankind from his tears as they fell to earth. He was also attributed with the creation of the intellect and higher reasoning. On cutting his phallus, perhaps in an act of circumcision, he is said to have drawn drops of blood that became *Hu* (authority) and *Sia* (the mind). *Sia* may well have represented the intuitive qualities of the mind as well as the power of the intellect.

The Journey of Re

The Egyptians equated the heavens with a stretch of water and imagined that the heavenly bodies travelled in barques that were not unlike the boats that they themselves created for travelling up and down the Nile. They were fascinated with the orbit of the sun and imagined that the sun god travelled across the sky in a solar barque. At nighttime it was imagined that Re travelled, in a second boat, through the underworld, illuminating each underworld cavern briefly as he passed by. The solar barque was thought to be made of gleaming gold and, in the Old Kingdom, Re was referred to as the 'great reed-floater'. Models of sun barques were placed in tombs so that the deceased would be able to participate in the voyage of Re.

The image of Re journeying through the underworld in a second barque inevitably created a link with Osiris. By association, Re became the ruler of the underworld, his passage bringing a moment of life to its inhabitants who then returned to a state of death when his vessel had moved on.

RE IN A READING

Upright

If you have chosen this stone tablet in a reading then there is an abundance of creative energy available to you at this time. You may experience this on a physical level, as energy returns to your body and your stamina or drive increases. You may be feeling renewed and discover that you have a desire to do new things or take a new interest in projects that you have avoided or neglected recently. On an emotional level you could well experience a sense of upliftment and release after a period of sadness or pain and feel your natural resilience re-emerging from within you. There is a great deal of joy to be found in the process of living and that joy is abundantly available to you now.

You may find yourself becoming the centre of attention for a while and this is appropriate for your development. Now is not a time to retreat from the world, succumb to modesty or hide your light. At the moment it is essential that you be seen. Success comes to you from being visible and available. Your presence is both inspiring to others and instrumental in furthering your own evolution. Your charismatic power is strong and you need to make the most of it. You may find that you have the gift of being in the right place at the right time as new doors begin to open up for you.

The stone of Re augurs a period of harmony; your popularity increases and you are better able to command the attention of other people. Perhaps you are taking a more central role in your family, amongst your friends or within the workplace. You are becoming a central pivot and the lives of others revolve around you. Your presence gives other people a reason to socialize or work together on a project that will benefit everyone. Let yourself emerge from past fears and self-doubt, and allow your radiance to bring to you the rewards and pleasures that you deserve.

Reversed

If this stone tablet is reversed then you may find yourself surrounded by interesting, charismatic people who are on a similar wavelength to yourself. This is a good time for making important new friends or for renewing special friendships that may have appeared to be on the decline in recent months. Sometimes we need a period of separation from our close companions in order that we, and they, may grow and develop. When the relationship is resumed it can do so from a new level of understanding, maturity and awareness. Your relationships as a whole will be particularly positive and fulfilling for you at this time. Other people enjoy being with you and what you learn from them will prove to be illuminating for you in return.

Alternatively, you may find yourself basking in reflected glory. Your children, parents, friends, colleagues or lovers are celebrating a success that enhances their reputation and, by association, it also enhances yours. You may be receiving direct acknowledgement for your support and input or you may just be gaining pleasure from seeing someone you care about succeed. Whatever the reason, this is a golden time that helps to reaffirm your value and strengthen your position in the world.

Attributes

If this stone tablet represents a person who has come into your life then they will be charismatic and attractive. He or she is often the centre of attention. This is a person who has a strong sense of purpose and direction. They are committed to their position in life and are loyal to their career or family role. Whilst kind, warm and generous, their agenda tends to come first and they are not easily deflected from their chosen course. This person is bigger than life, they are often the star of the show. The qualities of Re most strongly relate to the sign of Leo in western astrology.

Meditation

Close your eyes, breathe deeply and relax. Picture yourself with an unlimited source of sunlight, shining from within you. Imagine that you have a miniature sun at the base of your ribs that glows with inexhaustible light and energy. Imagine this energy spreading into any part of your body that needs to be strengthened or regenerated and see the light renewing and recharging you. Every part of you is filling with a sense of warmth and well-being and your image becomes radiant and attractive.

Visualize the golden sunlight radiating from you to transform your environment and your relationships. Your home is filled with your light, as is your place of work; everywhere you go you leave a trail of brilliance that transforms the atmosphere and inspires others to become more loving and creative. Your limitless light makes you magnetic to new, creative opportunities and constantly available for loving, supportive people.

POSITIVE AFFIRMATIONS

My creative potential is infinite.
It is safe for me to change and develop.
My warmth and beauty shine out for all to see.
I radiate strength, confidence and unlimited light.
I am filled with energy and enthusiasm.
I create myself anew each day.
I grow towards the light.

KHONSU

God of the Moon

— Wandering —

— Youthfulness —

— Pathways —

— Provision —

The god Khonsu is the youthful god of the moon. He is usually depicted as human, but being a god of the sky, he can also take the form of a hawk. He generally wears a long, tightly fitting robe and a necklace. Khonsu's head is shaven except for one temple which has a lock of hair that signifies youth and royalty. On his head he bears the crescent of the new moon that cradles the rounded image of the full moon. Accounts of his lineage vary. At Thebes he was thought to be the adopted child of the god Amun and his consort, Mut. The meaning of his name is 'wanderer' which refers to the path of the moon across the sky; and he was the navigator of human destinies. His colour is the silvery white of the moon.

Khonsu the Child

Khonsu is the epitome of youthful beauty. He is an archetype that represents the youthful wonder and spontaneity within us all. Like many children and young people, his radiance is increased by his lack of worldly knowledge. He is more beautiful because he is not conscious of his impact on the world around him. Like the moon following its divine course across the heavens, Khonsu is powerful because he just follows his divine path. He is simply being himself.

Although early accounts of Khonsu attribute him with a more aggressive, bloodthirsty nature, he is generally considered to be a gentle god with special therapeutic powers. His reputation was one of kindness and compassion. As childhood is the beginning of life, the image of the divine child in ancient Egypt was thought to contain the powerful seed of all future beginnings. The most worshipped figure of youth was the 'child Horus', although many other youthful deities were significant. Khonsu, like other child deities, represents the potential that we all have to fulfil our divine purpose and become all that we were created to be.

Khonsu the Navigator

As a moon god, Khonsu was seen as a wanderer and a navigator charting a course across the night sky. He was known as 'he who crosses the sky in a boat'. To the Egyptians, the moon was the 'sun that shines at night' and its journey was accompanied by adoring baboons and jackals. The association between baboons and the moon made this animal sacred to Khonsu. In one of his roles he was thought to chart individual destiny and calculate the life span. He certainly highlights the difference between human destiny and the divine purpose that underpins it.

We are free to make conscious choices about the paths that we take; there are numerous possible routes we can follow that will lead us to the achievement of our ultimate goals. However, when we listen to our underlying purpose and we are loyal to our true nature, the choices that we make can become more aligned to our higher destiny. When voyaging across water it is preferable to work with the currents rather than fighting against them. Khonsu reminds us to journey with innocent wonder and surrender to the divine plan that we have co-created with the universe. We always have a choice to chart the happiest course and travel in a state of grace.

Khonsu the Exorcist

The healing abilities of Khonsu include the powers of exorcism. His image was called upon to cast out demons and restore harmony. Sick and possessed people from all over Egypt and the territories beyond would invoke Khonsu to cleanse them of their inner conflicts. In one account, a statue of Khonsu was used to drive a demon from the body of a Syrian princess. Her grateful father then returned the statue to Egypt, amidst great pomp and celebration, together with rich offerings to the god for his service.

KHONSU IN A READING

Upright

If you have chosen this stone tablet in a reading then you could find yourself embarking on a journey, stepping out into the unknown or taking a new and unexpected route towards the goals you have set yourself. This is a time of youthful enthusiasm, experimentation, new adventure, joyfulness and divine innocence. Perhaps you are feeling younger and more energized than you have felt for a while and your confidence is strong enough for you to enjoy the game of life. Any world weariness is dissolving and you can enjoy your childlike nature. Those around you may well find you particularly attractive and fun to be with.

Your innocence is a strength, rather than a weakness. You are free of judgements or preconceptions that would limit your ability to act on positive opportunities. Cynicism will not serve you now; it will only dampen your joy and restrict your forward mobility. It is your innocence and not your cynicism that will protect you. Innocent fun can bring miraculous healing to your spirit and awaken your heart to the vibration of pure joy. What is more, if you are willing to drop the adult complications that you have created for yourself and view the world with the bright simplicity of a child, then you will be able to cast out the demons of worry, overthinking and excessive self-doubt.

The stone of Khonsu augurs a time of renewal and regeneration. When we have expended too much energy plotting, planning and attempting to control the course of our lives then we need to redress the balance by becoming spontaneous. There are moments when we will only progress if we are willing to take a spontaneous leap into the unknown, and this is one of them. The past is over, the future is not yet within your grasp; all you have to play with is the fun and freedom of the present moment. Please remember that Khonsu is both a wanderer and a navigator, so your route, although free and unrestricted, is never without its own divine plan.

Reversed

If this stone tablet is reversed then your spontaneity and good humour is challenging those around you to lighten up. Your influence cuts through the seriousness and pretension of adult life and creates new opportunities for everyone to enjoy themselves. Perhaps you are the life and soul of the party or perhaps you have just dropped your worldly cares and are assisting your family, friends or colleagues to do the same. At this time, you are compassionate to the needs and feelings of others and your natural, gentle wisdom creates the space for healing to occur.

Most people will enjoy your company at this time, but be aware that not everyone will be comfortable with your youthful enthusiasm, vivacity and kindness. For some, your liveliness and good humour will highlight the restrictions that they have placed on themselves and show them how dispirited they have become. To be compassionate to yourself it may be important to retreat from anyone who displays jealousy or resentment and allow your natural radiance to attract companions who can appreciate your spontaneous nature.

Attributes

If this stone tablet represents a person then they will either be quite young or eternally youthful. This person is very attractive; their freshness makes them highly appealing although their innocence may leave them totally unaware of the effect that they have on others. Their presence motivates you, even if they are a little demanding of your attention. They remind you to have fun and, like a holiday, they transport you from your daily routine and into a series of playful adventures. In western astrology the qualities of Khonsu most directly relate to the signs of Gemini and Cancer.

Meditation

Close your eyes, breathe deeply and relax. Visualize yourself as a young child. The exact age is up to you but do your best to see yourself at a time when you were uncluttered by adult responsibilities and restricted thinking. How did you look at that age? What clothes did you wear? Acknowledge any childhood challenges or disappointments that you had. If thinking about your childhood makes you feel sad or angry then accept those feelings. If your childhood memories are loving and joyful then acknowledge those feelings too. What did you love to do? What games or activities gave you pleasure?

When you have built a sense of your inner child, ask your child-self the following questions: *'What can I do to bring more joy into my life?' 'How can I free up and have more fun?'* Notice any thoughts, feelings or images that you receive and act upon your positive impulses.

POSITIVE AFFIRMATIONS

I enjoy my life.
I leap into the adventure of each new moment.
I am youthful, vibrant and alive.
I journey with hope, trust and positive anticipation.
I grow younger, healthier and more beautiful every day.
It is safe for me to be spontaneous.
I choose freedom and fun.

KHNUM

Creator of Life

— New Life —
— Language —
— Creativity —
— Procreation —

The god Khnum is often described as the creator of life. He is a ram god who fashions gods, men, birds, fish and cattle from clay before breathing the life force into his creations. He is a giver of health and his many gifts include the various languages of the human race. Khnum is often depicted with a humanoid body and a ram's head; frequently he is pictured sitting at his potter's wheel moulding new life from clay. The hieroglyph for his name is a ram's horn. At Esna, in the south of Egypt, Khnum was thought to be the creator of all things. He was imagined to embody the entire world and his divinity encompassed other deities such as Geb, Shu, Osiris and Re. His colours are violet and reddish gold.

Creator of New Life and Abundance

Khnum was the lord of the Nile cataracts. He controlled the annual inundation of the Nile from the caverns of Hapy, the god who embodied the Nile flood. The worship of Khnum, with appropriate financial contributions to his temple, was thought to assure the prosperity of Egypt.

Khnum was thought to preside over childbirth alongside the frog goddess, Heket. It was imagined that Khnum created each child on his potter's wheel, crafting it carefully from clay and planting it as a seed in the womb of its mother. He was a god of fertility and procreation who directed the cycles of life. He could bless the womb with new life, the land with new crop growth and the peoples of Egypt with prosperity and abundance.

In breathing new life into human progeny, Khnum is seen as a giver of health. He is also attributed with the creation of animals, birds, fish and even other deities. Khnum is perhaps representative of the creative process as well as the potential to create.

As a potter, a trade that the Egyptians would have easily identified with, he is the image of the practical craftsman who is able to direct his will and vision into creating something useful and tangible. His creativity was not abstract but direct. Khnum may be a creator god but he is also symbolic of the human ability to turn dreams into reality and he reminds us that spiritual evolution often comes through practical application and is available to us all.

The Symbology of the Ram

Khnum was the divine ram, the initial spark of creation, perhaps symbolic of the Arien age that preceded the Christian age of Pisces and our current age of Aquarius. Indeed 'Khnum' became the literal name for the ram, and Khnum bestowed the ram with sacred powers. The worship of Khnum included the burial of mummified rams at Elephantine, each decorated with a gilded head piece and placed in a sarcophagus.

It is not surprising that the ram was thought to have life-giving properties. It was a beast associated with male fertility and the power to procreate. Even today in western astrology the ram is a symbol of new life. The sign of Aries is the first of the twelve signs of the zodiac and it represents the energy that instigates creation and the fiery passion that is required to seed new growth.

The Consorts of Khnum

Khnum is said to have been assisted in his work by the goddesses Satis and Anukis. Satis was a guardian goddess of the southern borders of Egypt. She was thought to slay the enemies of the king with her arrows. Alongside Khnum, she was associated with the Nile inundation; she presented jars of water to the deceased for purification. The goddess Anukis was thought to be the child of Khnum and Satis although some accounts portray her as the wife of Khnum and mother of Satis. She was a goddess of the first Nile cataract at Aswan and she had a temple dedicated to her on the island of Seheil.

KHNUM IN A READING

Upright

If you have chosen this stone tablet in a reading then you are being blessed with the right amount of energy to stimulate the creative process in your life at this time. Think about your current projects and ask yourself what practical steps you need to take to facilitate or enhance their development. Do you have a vision of what you wish to create in your life? Are you collecting together the raw materials that will make your vision a reality? Are you fashioning those raw materials into their desired shape? Is it time to breathe life into your creations and allow them to live and grow on their own merits?

Whatever you need or desire to create, this is not a time to hold back or procrastinate. If you do not have a positive, future vision then you need to develop one. If you have the vision to do something new in your life but you have yet to take the practical steps that will ensure that your vision becomes a reality then this is the time to back up your dreams and move forward towards a tangible resolution of your goals. So many of us hold back because we fear failure or because we do not trust ourselves to handle the challenges and commitments that can come with the creative process. The only true failure comes with avoiding your growth and creative development. Success always comes when we listen to our dreams and desires and act upon them by taking the practical steps necessary to give them life.

The stone of Khnum augurs a time when you move from the abstract into the tangible. It indicates projects with good beginnings that can be developed to benefit all. Khnum blesses you with inspiration, health and prosperity. There could be the birth of a child, a new job, a new relationship, a new beginning for a business venture or creative endeavour. Everything bodes well for the future; you just need to have faith in yourself and act.

Reversed

If this stone tablet is reversed then you are instrumental in furthering the dreams and goals of other people. Perhaps you come up with an idea that gives someone else the initial impetus to begin a project or create a new business venture. Your input could even instigate a chain of events that has a positive effect on people and places that are currently unfamiliar to you. Certainly your words of wisdom encourage others to begin a path of spiritual or material growth. All areas of communication are important to you now. It would be a good time to learn a new language and prepare yourself for new relationships that are beyond your current circle of friends, colleagues and clients.

This is a prosperous time when any investment in the success of others will pay off for you. The investment may be a monetary one; you may provide seed money for someone else's project or support them financially so that they can carry out something that they have always wanted to do.

However, it is more likely to be an investment of time, energy and love that will return to you in abundance when you are the one who requires some practical help or creative encouragement.

Attributes

If this stone tablet represents a person who has come into your life then they could be an artist, a craftsperson or someone blessed with a multitude of creative abilities. He or she has the practical skills needed to put their ideas into action and the will-power and enthusiasm to make them work. This could be a natural instigator who is always at the forefront of new creative ventures, a new parent or someone who is going to embark upon a new business venture. Be happy for them and do your best to be supportive. If they succeed in their venture then you may benefit in unexpected ways. In western astrology the qualities of Khnum most directly relate to the sign of Aries.

Meditation

Close your eyes, breathe deeply and relax. Picture yourself with a lump of rich, raw clay and imagine yourself modelling it into a rough human shape. The clay is soft against your hands and it is easy for you to model. Within your imagination see yourself transforming the shape into a perfect representation of yourself, and as you do, think about all of the things that you would like to create or change in your life. If you would like to be fitter, healthier or happier, then imagine yourself breathing life into this statue and endowing it with fitness, health and happiness. If you wish to be more creative, prosperous and successful then visualize yourself breathing these qualities into your image of clay. If you wish to grow spiritually then bless your figure with the potential for spiritual evolution. When you are complete, visualize this figure coming to life and imagine these new qualities and strengths coming to life inside you.

POSITIVE AFFIRMATIONS

My talents grow and multiply.
I give generously and receive in abundance.
It is easy for me to learn new things.
I communicate clearly and effectively.
I easily breathe life into new projects and new relationships.
I create prosperity for myself and others.
I am practical and creative.

HAPY

God of the Flooded Nile

— Fullness —

— Abundance —

— Fluidity —

— Ebb and Flow —

The god Hapy is the personification of the yearly flooding of the Nile. His dwelling place was in the caverns of the Nile cataracts, an area presided over by the ram god Khnum. He is depicted in human form with aquatic plants upon his head and bearing offerings. His abundant prosperity is represented by a paunch and hanging breasts. He was a god without a temple or a sanctuary built in his honour but he commanded great respect because of the prosperous fertility that he brought to the land. Hapy was a benign deity who blessed the Egyptian people with their livelihood. Although a male god, his sweet nature was quite maternal. The colours of Hapy are the greens of Nile water and vegetation.

The Prosperity of Hapy

Hapy was a prosperous god whose abundance was symbolized by the fullness of his body. His image was one of plentiful celebration, enrichment and fulfilment. He embodied the yearly flooding of the Nile that left deposits of fertile silt upon the land, rich in minerals and nutrients that helped the crops to grow strong and plentiful. Hapy was the ebb and flow of the Nile. He was the season of fertility and the giver of gifts.

Hapy was one of a number of Egyptian gods who, although predominantly male, were portrayed as being quite androgynous. He has been described as having the breasts of a nurse and he may well have represented some of the nurturing qualities that are inherent in us all. In a way, the Nile must have seemed like a nurturing benefactor to the Egyptians, who relied on it for survival. It was the source of life and a constant provider of food and raw materials.

The Life of the Nile

The plant and animal life within and around the Nile delta was sacred to Hapy. The fish of the Nile and the fowl of the Nile marshes were all dedicated to him. His entourage was said to include a number of crocodile gods and he was thought to have a harem of frog goddesses. The plants associated with Hapy were the papyrus and the lotus. The Nile god was often depicted with a headdress of plants and sometimes he was given two forms signifying his presence in both Lower and Upper Egypt; one form bore the papyrus of the north and the other bore the lotus of the south. Hapy was often shown semi-naked or dressed in a similar fashion to the boatmen and fishermen who navigated the Nile waters, with his full stomach overhanging his narrow belt.

Hapy inhabited the Nile cataracts, areas of dramatic waterfall which cause the river to descend rapidly from source to mouth. It was thought that he lived on the Isle of Bigeh near the first Nile cataract. From his cavern he poured water from his sacred urns; some he poured to the heavens and some he distributed to the earth. The Egyptians generally believed that the source of the Nile was Nu, the primordial waters that filled the void before and beyond the existence of the world, although worshippers of Osiris also imagined the yearly Nile flood to be the tears of Isis as she mourned for her murdered husband.

The Worship of Hapy

There were no temples built to honour Hapy although his image frequently appeared in temples dedicated to the worship of other gods. He was often depicted bearing a tray or table of rich offerings to the chief deity of the temple. These offerings would be gleaned from the abundant Nile delta.

Each June, the Egyptians would offer up their gifts to Hapy. By honouring him, they hoped to win his favour and ensure that the Nile inundation reached the ideal height to fertilize the land by around the middle of the month. Their offerings included the singing of poetic hymns and incantations.

HAPY IN A READING

Upright

If you have chosen this stone tablet in a reading then this could be a period of rich fertility in your life if you allow it to be. Often the fertility comes with a willingness to receive it. The universe delights in sending us gifts of love, prosperity and healing but it is up to us to learn how to be available for the abundance that is around us. We learn many negative or limiting expectations about the world. We wish our lives away, worrying about what we do not have rather than blessing and enjoying the wealth of each new experience and giving thanks for the love that we have already created. Bless every gift that you receive, each friendly smile, every word of love and every pay cheque! Regularly tell yourself that you deserve the best things in life and that you are willing to receive love, joy and prosperity in abundance.

It is possible that your emotions are particularly fluid and powerful at this time, with acute highs and lows; but you are probably feeling more alive because of it. Even if your life is challenging or busy you may find that you are feeling generally satisfied with your lot. This is a productive phase when projects will have good beginnings and stand every chance of coming to fruition.

The stone of Hapy generally augurs a time of fullness and abundance when many good things are happening and rich opportunities are available to us spiritually, materially and emotionally. However, Hapy also reminds us of the cycle of ebb and flow. For everything in our lives there is a season. If our lives are full of abundant opportunities, we need to celebrate them and do our best to make the most of them. If our lives go through a fallow period when nothing appears to be happening, then we can use that time to enjoy the simplicity of each new moment, hone our skills for the future and meditate upon our inner guidance. Joy comes from a balance of stillness and activity. Love and prosperity both flow more easily when we are willing to adapt to change.

Reversed

If this stone tablet is reversed then you are being asked to acknowledge yourself for the care, love and abundance that you give to others, and you are reminded to look more closely at how your good fortune can be of greater benefit.

If you are feeling particularly loved or loving then sharing your love with somebody else will allow it to grow. The giving of love can include praise, acknowledgements, compliments and words of encouragement. If you are feeling particularly prosperous then consider how your prosperity could benefit the people you love or create something positive within the wider community in which you live.

It is not valid to give from a sense of guilt. We truly deserve every good thing that we receive and we benefit no one by feeling guilty about our good fortune. Instead, it is important that we give from a sense of celebration and a trust that what we give to others will benefit everyone concerned. The energy of prosperity grows when it is constantly flowing and diminishes when it is static or held back. What flows from us with a good will and a good heart will ultimately flow back to us in countless ways.

Attributes

If this stone tablet represents a person who has come into your life then he or she will be a caring, supportive influence. This is someone who responds to any situation with receptivity, sensitivity and emotion rather than with logic. They are sympathetic and perceptive, able to be attentive to the needs of other people. The presence of this person is fortunate and may bring about prosperity or rich opportunities for spiritual growth and personal advancement. In western astrology the qualities of Hapy most directly relate to the sign of Pisces.

Meditation

Close your eyes, breathe deeply and relax. In your mind, declare that you are willing to receive and share the abundance of Hapy. Think about what you would like to give and receive at this time. Whom could you give more love to? Who would benefit from your positive, loving attention, praise, encouragement or reassurance? What practical help could you offer? Whom could you benefit with a gift of prosperity? This does not need to be money; it could be the sharing of a skill, a shared meal or the passing on of wisdom. Picture yourself giving gladly. Then, think about what you would like to receive in your life and imagine yourself easily receiving the gifts of love and prosperity that you desire. If you wish for something beautiful, imagine yourself touching it. If you wish for love, imagine that your heart is touched by it. When you complete this meditation, begin the process of giving and affirm your willingness to receive.

POSITIVE AFFIRMATIONS

I am always fed and nourished.
I am willing to receive the support that I need.
My life is filled with gifts.
I deserve the best things in life.
Abundant prosperity constantly flows into my life.
Love flows to me and around me wherever I go.
I easily adapt to change.

MAAT

Goddess of Cosmic Harmony

— Truth —

— Justice —

— Morality —

— Integrity —

The goddess Maat is often depicted as a woman wearing an ostrich feather on her head, or sometimes she is symbolized by the ostrich feather alone. Normally Maat is shown standing although, on occasions, she is winged and sitting on her heels. Pharaohs invested themselves with the right to govern by claiming that their rulership upheld the laws of the universe that Maat embodied. The wisdom of this goddess was crucial to the assessment of the dead, allowing those with a blameless life to enter paradise. Her influence rules legal matters and creates sound judgement, maintaining order and balance in the world. The existence of Maat made life, and continuing life after death, possible. Her colours are whites and mauves.

Cosmic Order and Justice

The goddess Maat is the embodiment of the order and balance within all things. She became known as a daughter of the sun god Re and was said to be 'at the nostrils of Re'; perhaps indicating that the laws of creation and the laws of cosmic harmony are inextricably linked. Maat was thought to be the wife of Thoth, the judge of the gods, and she represented the human qualities of fairness, judgement and legality, as well as the forces of divine order. She provided a structure and a substance that underpinned the nature of all creation. Perhaps this was why she was also described as the 'food and drink of Re'.

The name of Maat and the qualities associated with her became an essential part of law and justice for the ancient Egyptians. Judges were known as priests of Maat, and Pharaohs associated themselves with her, declaring themselves to be representative of divine order. Maat was one of a number of gods who invested the Pharaoh with the right to rule and to engage in the mortal tasks of government and law making.

Maat in the Hall of Judgement

Maat is often depicted fulfilling an essential role in the Hall of Judgement. After someone died, it was believed that his or her soul passed through the Hall of Judgement for assessment before moving on into the underworld. The jackal god Anubis would weigh the heart of the deceased on 'the scales of Maat' before Osiris and the council of forty-two judges. On the other side of the scales was placed 'the feather of Maat' which, in itself, symbolized truth. It is interesting that the Egyptians equated truth, honesty and goodness with the lightness of a feather, imagining a person with a truthful soul to be light-hearted. If the deceased had lived a good, honest life then the scales would balance; if not then the heart would weigh heavily against the feather.

The heart itself was a symbol of life. The body was thought to die because the heart had grown weary. It was an organ that was generally left within the body during the embalming process despite the fact that the other internal organs were removed for preservation in a series of jars. The probable reason for this was that the heart was thought to be essential for the continuation of life after death. To aid the deceased with the process of judgement, a 'heart scarab' amulet was placed within the wrappings of the mummy in the hope that it would prevent the heart from giving an unfavourable report of the person's life. The heart was representative of the person's character, including his or her emotions and intellect.

The Scales of Maat

The image of the scales still symbolizes law, order and the process of justice in the modern world. The symbol turns up again and again as an international emblem of the legal system. In western astrology, Libra, the sign of higher reason and justice, is also symbolized by the scales. Perhaps this is not surprising as modern astrology has its origins in the Middle East and North Africa.

MAAT IN A READING

Upright

If you have chosen this stone tablet in a reading then this is a reminder that divine order will prevail regardless of our human whims or personal dramas. Nature is always looking to create balance, and true spiritual justice exists even when the world appears to be unfair. So many of us learn to fear the process of justice. We may grow up with limiting beliefs about a punishing god or a social hierarchy that is poised to stamp upon ordinary people regardless of whether they are innocent or guilty. In reality, divine justice is based upon love, acceptance and fairness. The natural order of the universe delights in lifting us upwards towards our highest joy; liberating us from our fears and our self-imposed limitations.

The divine order is compassionate, merciful and supportive. By working against the nature of the universe we may create struggle, frustration and hardship. However, by working with the universal intelligence, we can learn to operate in a state of grace. Maat blesses us with forgiveness. She indicates that we would benefit from forgiving other people, forgiving ourselves and letting go of past injustice. She also teaches us to be objective and impartial because true compassion is born from true objectivity.

The stone of Maat augurs a time when we can take our rightful place in the scheme of things. The past is over; the future is, as yet, a blank page in an open book. It is the present that we may look to for our salvation. It does not matter what has happened to us; our past injustices are far gone and our fears for the future are just illusions. We are free to create the reality that we choose from this moment onwards.

Reversed

If this stone tablet is reversed then you are being asked to provide a balanced judgement or assessment that will aid the progress of another person. You will need to act with clarity, honesty and integrity. You may even be called on to make rapid decisions, but do your best not to get flustered or be pushed into proceeding before you are ready. Your fairness and compassion can breathe new life into a situation, heal a relationship or bring fresh hope to someone who was beginning to lose faith in themselves. Your grace, symmetry and level headedness bring inspiration and reassurance.

Alternatively, your influence provides balance. You could be the perfect person to complete a team; balancing out the other personalities involved to create an effective professional unit or harmonious family group. Your presence is calming and helps to coax others out of extremes of mood or behaviour and into a more constructive state of mind. You may even find that you create balance by being a brilliant negotiator, agent or diplomat who calms the air between two or more parties. This balancing role is strongly placed and very fortunate for you at this time, but if you find that providing divine order for others brings you personal disorder and disharmony then you need to be more detached and let others take greater responsibility for themselves.

Attributes

If this stone tablet represents a person who has come into your life then they will be fair, impartial and well balanced. She or he will be an excellent negotiator and a good judge of character. Although sensitive, this is not someone who is ruled by passion or given to great displays of emotion; rather they tend to keep their feelings hidden, preferring to operate as objectively as possible in most situations. They enjoy the finer things in life: good friendships, fine literature, sweet music and the arts. They are constantly striving for harmony within their relationships and will exercise great tact and diplomacy to this end. The qualities of Maat are most directly linked to the sign of Libra in western astrology.

Meditation

Close your eyes, breathe deeply and relax. Think about areas of resentment, imbalance or injustice in your life, past or present. In your mind, ask Maat to release you from the effects of injustice. Visualize your body, mind and emotions filling with the white or mauve light of Maat. Imagine this light dissolving your resentment and correcting any imbalance so that you may create your life anew, uncluttered by negative expectations. Picture Maat releasing you from relationships or situations that no longer serve you, breaking your connection to anyone who treats you unfairly. Imagine yourself free to develop new, fair and honest relationships with people better able to respect your needs and wishes. As any resentment, disappointment or sadness melts away, picture your heart growing lighter and brighter. See yourself becoming more joyful. Your balance and awareness allows you to view others with fairness, compassion and objectivity.

POSITIVE AFFIRMATIONS

I am healthy and balanced.
I am always in a state of grace.
It is easy for me to see all sides of a situation.
The divine order of the universe supports me in health and happiness.
It is easy for me to be fair, honest and impartial.
My life is balanced, within and without.
My life is harmonious.

KHEPRI

Scarab Beetle of the Sun

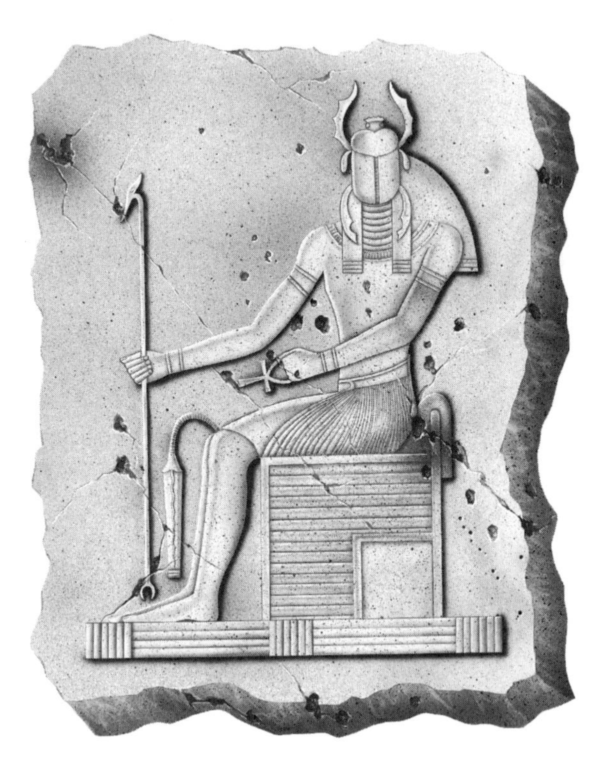

— Emergence —

— Motivation —

— Propulsion —

— Adornment —

The Egyptians were fascinated with the scarab beetle and its habit of rolling balls of dung across the ground. They likened this exercise to the propulsion of the sun on its circuit across the sky. Khepri is the sun god and creator in the form of a scarab. He was imagined to be created of his own accord rather than undergoing the natural cycle of reproduction, and he represented the initial spark of creation. Khepri was usually depicted as a dung beetle but he could also be portrayed as a hawk-winged beetle or as a man with the head of a scarab. Sometimes he was linked to another aspect of the sun god by depictions that show him with the head of a ram. The colours of Khepri are black, blue and gold.

The Scarab and the Sun

It was the image of dung beetles rolling balls of dung ahead of themselves that provided the Egyptians with a symbol for the passage of the sun across the heavens. They imagined that the sun was transported in a similar way, pushed along by a beetle. In addition, beetles were observed to emerge from balls of dung as if by magic. This image was not dissimilar to the concept of the creator god Atum and his later counterpart, the sun god Re, emerging, self-created, from the waters of Nu at the beginning of time. The beetle became inextricably linked with the sun and sun worship, and the scarab god Khepri became one face of the all powerful sun god.

The reality of the dung beetle, however, is much simpler and more down to earth than this heavenly notion. The beetles burrow holes to store their dung, so that they and their larvae can feed on it. The practice of collecting and rolling balls of dung is part of this creature's ongoing cycle of survival.

The Youthful Sun

Because scarab beetles appeared to materialize from dung, Khepri became associated with the sun as it surfaced from below the eastern horizon at dawn. His was the face of the morning sun of the east emerging from the underworld and, as such, he was an image of youthfulness. Khepri was linked to new life, rebirth and renewed vigour. An additional connection between the image of the scarab and the creator god Atum comes from a reference to Khepri creating the earth from his spittle. The veneration of the image of a dung beetle into the sacred sun scarab, Khepri, is an excellent example of how the ancient Egyptians sought to find explanations for the workings of the universe and derived spiritual meaning from the natural world. In doing so, they have left us with a unique metaphor for the divine spark within all life.

The Uses of the Scarab

In ancient Egypt, scarab-beetle figures were used for adornment and as totems in sacred ritual and funerary practices. Scarabs were often carved from anthracite or soapstone but they could also be cut from semi-precious minerals or moulded from clay. During life and after death, a scarab was often worn as an amulet to bring good fortune to the wearer. In addition, scarabs were used as administrative seals by Egyptian officials and they often carried important information in hieroglyphic writing on the underside. Some scarabs bore the names of royalty, while others had spells written on them.

Heart scarabs were used to aid the journey of the deceased into the underworld by helping to ensure that their heart gave a favourable account of their character in the Hall of Judgement. The placing of a heart scarab within the wrappings of the mummified body, or within the tomb, was a totem of new life, and it was imagined that the deceased would rise again like the sun in the morning or emerge into a new world like the creator god from the chaos of Nu.

KHEPRI IN A READING

Upright

If you have chosen this stone tablet in a reading then this is a time of new motivation. You are being supported to move beyond any fear or procrastination. You may feel motivated to pursue or complete a project you had lost faith in, or perhaps your courage to be out in the world fulfilling your purpose has re-emerged after a period of self-doubt. If a lack of motivation still clouds your horizon, look inside yourself for the underlying fear or resistance so that you can acknowledge it, deal with it and put it aside. It is important to progress now; you will benefit from your commitment and persistence.

You may discover that commitment and hard work are two very different things. Putting energy into a project or a relationship and doing what is needed to make it succeed is quite different from the old work ethics that many of us have learnt. We often believe that we have to work hard to achieve every small success and our expectations can turn even the simplest task into a struggle. The belief in hard work is often what keeps us from gaining pleasure, prosperity and joy. It creates a barrier that opportunity and fulfilment cannot penetrate. Developing a belief in ease and combining it with positive energy and commitment to our goals can open doors and create miracles.

The stone of Khepri augurs a time of energy, drive and determination. We may discover that our tasks are much easier than we imagined and we may enjoy ourselves so much that we do not experience any hardship. Contrary to popular opinion, our commitment can liberate us. Even the simplest or lowliest of tasks can raise us to the level of the divine if we allow them to. You can either choose to view yourself as a dung beetle endlessly rolling your pile of dung over the dirt or you could see yourself as Khepri, making a journey of glory, commitment and spiritual purpose across the heavens.

Reversed

If this stone tablet is reversed then you have become the motivating force for another person. Perhaps someone aspires to be like you and they are willing to follow a career path, embark on a spiritual journey or voyage forth on a personal odyssey so that they may attain a similar position or status to your own. Alternatively, there is someone who loves you so much that they are willing to make career or personal changes that will provide you with a better standard of living, more practical help or greater love and support. You may be actively encouraging others or you may need to do nothing except be yourself, and provide the focus that they need to transform their life for the better.

Choosing Khepri reversed is also indicative of moving into a job or spiritual role that engages you in the motivation of other people. You could be teaching valuable skills, managing a team or commissioning others to provide a service. Your guiding influence brings benefits for all concerned. If you motivate other people with love rather than with fear then their loyalty will be greater, their progress more rapid and their commitment long lasting. You will be rewarded many times over and love will return to adorn you with true spiritual fulfilment.

Attributes

If this stone tablet represents a person then he or she will be self-contained, purposeful and strong. They may not, at first sight, seem remarkable but as they go about their work or fulfil their role within the community then they become the inevitable focus of attention. They gain visibility as one of the truly exceptional souls who benefit us all with their commitment and simple brilliance. When they operate from their underlying purpose then their charisma increases and they become the motivating force for everyone around them. The qualities of Khepri are most directly related to the signs of Capricorn and Leo in western astrology.

Meditation

Close your eyes, breathe deeply and relax. Picture yourself going about your daily affairs: travelling to work perhaps, washing the dishes, cleaning your home, paying the bills, answering the telephone; undertaking the many regular tasks that are part of looking after yourself and your family. Imagine each task becoming special. Everything that you do becomes blessed with sacred power.

Picture a guiding light around you that illuminates and enhances the beauty in everything you do. Visualize yourself with additional energy to complete tasks joyfully and efficiently, leaving you with time for yourself. When you complete this meditation think of something practical you can do to make an everyday activity sacred. Perhaps you could bathe or eat your dinner by candle light, or tell someone that you love them, or one of an infinite number of simple things that can make an ordinary moment touch the divine.

POSITIVE AFFIRMATIONS

My life gets easier all the time.
It is easy for me to motivate myself.
My spiritual purpose guides me onwards and upwards.
My honest dedication brings me glory and recognition.
My commitment brings me bountiful rewards.
I am fired up and inspired.
Life is simple and easy.

ANAT

Warrior Goddess

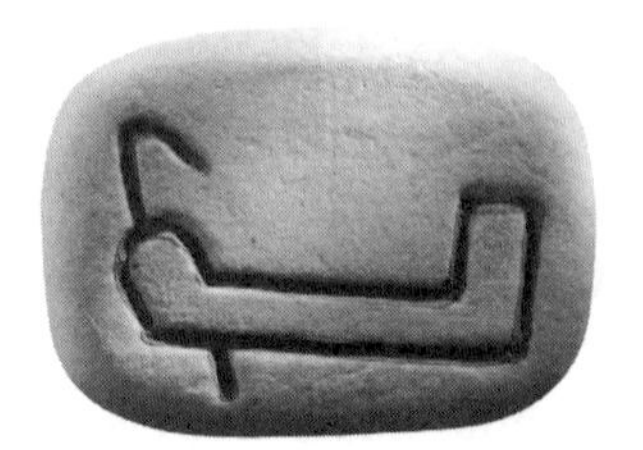

— Courage —

— Fearlessness —

— Vigour —

— Sexuality —

The goddess Anat originated on the coast of Syria and her influence extended into Egypt. She is depicted with a high crown flanked with plumes and she carries the shield, lance and battle axe of combat. The forearm and stick hieroglyph on her stone tablet signifies strength and action. Some legends cast Anat as one of the wives of Seth while others portray her as a sister and sexual partner of Baal, god of stormy weather. She was seen as a protectress and had the courage and determination of an avenging angel. Anat was also viewed as a fertility goddess and in this aspect she was linked to the fertility god Min. Her connection with life-blood was indicative of her ability to bring prosperity to the land and the peoples who worshipped her. Her colour is red.

Anat the Outsider

Anat was one of a number of foreign deities whose influence extended into Egyptian territory. She was primarily a fertility goddess who was thought to sprinkle the dew and bring forth fresh-water springs from the earth. Together with her brother and consort, Baal, she was portrayed as a bloodthirsty goddess with a love of battle and conquest.

Anat's cult spread across the Egyptian borders and grew in popularity, eventually becoming actively promoted. With Baal and their sister Astarte, Anat was given a place within the Egyptian pantheon. In the contest between Seth and Horus for the throne of Egypt, Anat and Astarte were offered to Seth as wives as an appeasement to the god of chaos when the judgement went against him. They replace Nephthys, Seth's original consort who left his side out of loyalty to their murdered brother Osiris. Anat also became associated with the goddess Hathor, who was often linked to foreign deities and who was also reputed to have a vengeful, bloodthirsty side to her nature, although this was often subdued.

Anat the Warrior

The peoples of the ancient world had a need for warrior gods and goddesses. The conquest of new territories and the disputes between the rulers of emerging nations were an important part of the process of civilization. The indigenous gods of Egypt were believed to be instrumental in the success of Egyptian campaigns into neighbouring lands; so the adoption of warrior gods from other territories would not have been completely alien to Egyptian culture and beliefs. It is not surprising that the concerns of ancient peoples, particularly those who were situated in close geographical proximity to one another, would have had strong similarities. The symbolism of gods and goddesses was inextricably linked to the need to explain the forces of the natural world and the preoccupation with basic survival.

Anat, Astarte and Baal

Anat had some similarities to her sister goddess, Astarte, a deity of both love and war. The two goddesses were invested with a fiery passion that could equally bring about new life or create destruction. They were the embodiment of the raw energy of creation and evolution, a force that can be unstable if it is not correctly channelled. Astarte became associated with chariots, horses and the attainment of equestrian skills.

Baal was a god of the sky and of storms. It is perhaps the association with stormy weather and thunder that creates comparisons between Baal and Seth. However, the story of Baal is not dissimilar to the legend of Osiris. When Baal was murdered by Mot, a deity personifying death and barrenness, it was Anat who resurrected him from the underworld, giving him new life and wreaking revenge by slaying his murderer. Within a continuous cycle of death and rebirth, a victory for Baal would herald a period of fertility, while a victory for Mot would indicate drought and famine.

ANAT IN A READING

Upright

If you have chosen this stone tablet in a reading then this is a time to stand up for your rights, promote yourself and be fearless in pursuing new goals or defending your territory. The teaching of Anat is not one of compromise or diplomacy but rather it teaches the constructive use of aggressive energy. If you have become too passive in defending what is rightfully yours then it is time to become fired up with passion and make sure that your voice is heard. If you have the courage to use it, your passion can move mountains; it can win campaigns and promote your influence positively and effectively. If you fear your passion, resisting its call and squashing its power, then other people will invade your boundaries, disrupt your life and clutter your sacred space. Alternatively, it could build inside you until it becomes destructive aggression that leaks out in inappropriate ways when the pressure becomes too great to bear.

If you want your voice to be heard then you need to learn to use it. By assertively and clearly stating your case and being straightforward about your intentions, you give other people the information they need to respond to your wishes constructively. If you use your voice positively, allowing your passionate enthusiasm to inspire and stimulate others into action, then it becomes a powerful force for change in the world. Your ideas and opinions are valuable; do your best to express them fully and honestly.

Anat augurs a time of strength, energy and direct, positive action. If used constructively, this can be a very successful period when you have the energy that you need to get your life moving again. You have the drive to step out on your own and turn your life into a wonderful adventure. It is a good time to exercise, channelling any excess energy into dance, sports or an effective new fitness programme. Whatever you choose to do, trust your passion; it will awaken your creativity, keep you in touch with your divine purpose and help you to feel alive.

Reversed

If this stone tablet is reversed then you may find yourself supporting someone else to take direct, passionate action. Perhaps your enthusiasm has stirred them up into taking a positive risk that will change their life for the better; or perhaps the strength of your voice has reminded them that they too have a powerful voice to use. However, do make sure that you are not pushing someone into something that they genuinely do not want to do. If you are pushing hard to get another person to change then it may be valuable to examine your motives. Perhaps it is you who needs to be making changes and transforming your life for the better.

All of your relationships will be particularly fertile and creative at this time. You fire other people up and they, in turn, seem to stimulate your passion and enthusiasm. Please remember to use this energy constructively. It is there to remove obstacles from your life and get you moving again; it is not there to fuel pointless conflicts or subdue others into submission. Remember, the constructive use of passion is a wonderful gift of love that you can give to yourself and to other people.

Attributes

If this stone tablet represents a person who has come into your life then they will have a forceful presence. She or he could be from another country or have strong connections to other parts of the world. Alternatively, they may be a stranger to your life or have origins that are outside your normal circle or sphere of influence. Their energy and drive might seem to be a little shocking or radical at first but they are loyally supportive of your goals, rights and dreams. This woman or man could become a powerful ally. The qualities of Anat are most directly related to the sign of Aries in western astrology.

Meditation

Close your eyes, breathe deeply and relax. Picture yourself with the shield and the lance of Anat, marking out your sacred territory. In your mind's eye, see yourself standing on rich, fertile earth and drawing a wide circle around you with the point of the lance. Ask Anat to bless you with protection and to keep you safe inside this sacred space. Know that this sacred space is moveable: it travels with you wherever you go; and imagine that the shield gives you the power to protect yourself whenever you are feeling vulnerable or insecure. Know that you can shield yourself in ways that are positive and constructive for all concerned.

Next, imagine the energy of your life force growing. Picture yourself harnessing your passionate energy and creating the joy, freedom, health and exhilaration that you truly deserve. Know that you can channel it into the projects, relationships and experiences that will bring you the most happiness.

POSITIVE AFFIRMATIONS

I am safe with my passion.
It is safe for me to stand up for myself.
My passion awakens me to the joy and power of being alive.
My enthusiasm brings me friends and numerous rewards.
It is easy for me to speak up for myself.
I effectively assert my needs and desires.
I claim my sacred space.

MIN

God of Fertility

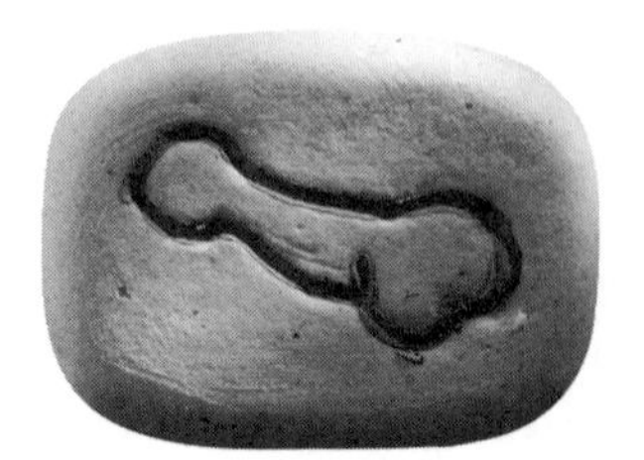

— Sexuality —

— Fruitfulness —

— Renewal —

— Regeneration —

The god Min represents sexual procreation. His fertility and blatant sexual power are often shown by depicting him with an erect phallus projecting outwards at a right angle to his body. He protected the eastern desert and is sometimes shown with his right arm raised and carrying the royal whip, poised to destroy his enemies. On his head is a crown of two high plumes and a long, hanging ribbon. Min has some similarities to the Greek god, Pan, and he could have been his forerunner. Like Pan, he is a nature spirit who celebrates the fertility of the earth and the free sexuality of all living things. He is associated with fertile vegetation and thunder. The colours of Min are orange, yellow and green.

Sexuality and Fruitfulness

Min is the embodiment of sexuality and the fruitfulness within all things. His erect phallus, while indicative of human sexuality, is also a symbol of the abundant fertility within nature. Originally Min was worshipped as a fetish that was shaped liked a jagged arrow. This fetish could have been symbolic of male and female organs in sexual union, although it is sometimes interpreted as a bolt of lightning. This image evolved into an emblem that was thought to be representative of the god when included in the design and decoration of other artifacts.

In earlier accounts, Min was related to the fertility and procreation of animals, but later he became more associated with the fertility of vegetation. Flowers were offered to Min in the belief that he would bring rich harvests to the Nile valley. The lettuce became the sacred plant of Min. It was thought to be an aphrodisiac and was imagined to greatly increase the sexual performance of the fertility god. At feasts and festivals in honour of Min, his priests would carry a variety of long lettuce, and depictions of the god often included the image of this plant. This strong association with lettuce may have been due to a sap it produced, reminiscent of human semen.

God of the East

Min was thought to provide protection for the mining regions in the eastern desert and it is perhaps because of this that he became associated with the god Horus, who was linked to the eastern delta and the route into Palestine. Some traditions combined them as Min-Horus and, by association, Isis was thought to be Min's mother. However, Min also bears some similarity to Osiris, who was another god linked to fertile vegetation, and some accounts describe Min in Osiris's role as husband of Isis and father of Horus.

Min could be invoked to protect mining expeditions. One of his sacred sites was at Quift, a small town and staging post for the mining explorations of the eastern desert region. He was a god of roads, who could look after anyone travelling through the desert and, like Horus, he was a 'lord of foreign lands'. His cult appears to have been quite strong and well organized. He was worshipped at a number of sites and there was a temple dedicated to Min at Akhmim. The Greeks, who associated him with their god Pan, called this site 'Panopolis'.

Masculine and Feminine

Although Min was quite obviously depicted as a male god, the qualities of sexuality and fertility that he embodied were both male and female. Like Pan and other nature gods, he celebrated the sexual power within all living things, and that included the feminine principle. It was only with later, patriarchal religions that the goddess became subjugated and suppressed. In ancient Egypt, the power of the goddess was very strong and was well represented by a number of prominent goddesses as well as by the nature of male gods who embraced the combined creative principle of masculine and feminine.

MIN IN A READING

Upright

If you have chosen this stone tablet in a reading then this is a time for enjoying the sexual power of your body and the transformational power of your spirit. It is appropriate to drop any worries or restrictions that you have burdened yourself with recently and to allow yourself some moments of uninhibited pleasure and indulgence. This is a period for celebrating, feasting, loving and lovemaking. Remember that it is good to be alive and let go of any fear or guilt that threatens to impede your enjoyment. Your body is special. It does not have to fit modern stereotypes of beauty and desirability in order to give you pleasure and to support you in health and well-being. If you love and accept your body exactly as it is and do your best to take care of it, it will respond with improved health, greater energy and an increased capacity for sensual ecstasy.

This may be a time for taking a new lover or for rekindling the sexual and emotional passions that are still smouldering away within a long-term relationship. Love yourself enough to communicate your sexual and emotional needs, and be as sensitive as you can to the needs of your partner. Good sexual communication takes practice but it is an essential part of lovemaking in an age of safer sex. Love yourself and your partner enough to play safely. The intimacy that comes from honesty and mutual care can take you to new areas of sexual freedom and new heights of passion.

The stone of Min augurs a period of spiritual alchemy when your enjoyment of life is the most instrumental part of your spiritual evolution. Do your best to love, laugh, live and learn. The best learning always comes through pleasure. The new lover in your life could be you. It is likely that you are feeling so good in your body and so much better about life in general that the sensual pleasure you experience comes from the pure joy of being yourself. You may want to move, dance, sing, dress up or pamper your body. Do it all. Life was meant to be a holiday!

Reversed

If this stone tablet is reversed then be aware that you are awakening the sexuality or sexual interest of another. This does not necessarily mean that you will become the focus of unwanted attention. Rather, it is indicative of your potency at this time that you can stimulate other people to remember their sexual, sensual or spiritual nature and that you can encourage them to celebrate the joy of being alive.

Alternatively, your influence may be helping to regenerate a project or rekindle a relationship between other people that appeared to have dwindled or died out completely. You could help to provide the funding, the energy, the advice or the practical assistance that gets things moving again. Your example may stimulate others to realize that there is something still worth working for and that there is always something worth celebrating. The death of one creative phase always leaves us with the seeds to begin a regeneration and to stimulate a process of rebirth. Your words, deeds or intentions can stimulate the fallow ground so that others may germinate those seeds, nurture new growth and harvest the fruits of past endeavours.

Attributes

If this stone tablet represents a person who has come into your life then they will be fun and flirtatious and more than a little seductive. He or she could easily display intense, powerful emotions and their lives may appear to be uncluttered by areas of self-doubt. This could be someone who has recently returned to life after a period of inactivity or seclusion and they may be keen to celebrate their newly regained energy and drive. The personality traits highlighted by Min most directly relate to the sign of Scorpio in western astrology.

Meditation

Close your eyes, breathe deeply and relax. Picture your body and imagine that there is a spiral of reddish-orange light that spins upwards from your groin to your navel. With every breath you take visualize the light growing stronger and the spiral spinning upwards with greater energy and intention.

After a while, the spiral multiplies and a number of new spirals spin away from your navel and travel outwards to different areas of your body, filling every part of you with healing energy, vitality and new life. In your mind's eye, the spirals become a multitude of bright new colours that help to regenerate and rejuvenate you. In the process, they safely reawaken your sexual power and stimulate you with the energy to transform your life for the better. Imagine these spirals of light sowing the seeds of spiritual evolution within every cell of your body and providing you with the energy to allow them to grow and multiply.

POSITIVE AFFIRMATIONS

I am safe with my sexuality.
I enjoy the sensuality of my body.
My life is filled with love and pleasure.
I love and appreciate my body.
I give myself permission to have fun.
My spirit is constantly evolving.
I live, love, learn and grow.

HEKET

Frog Goddess

— Birth —

— Midwifery —

— Quickening —

— The Home —

The goddess Heket was the divine midwife of ancient Egypt, the protector of new life. She was often depicted as a frog or as a woman with the head of a frog. Heket was frequently invoked to bring protection to the process of childbirth, or to defend the family unit and guard the home. Amulets and scarabs worn by women to protect them during the birthing process often bore her image, and she was also believed to bring relief to the mother. The influence of Heket was said to bring the first signs of life, or the quickening, to the unborn child, and to hasten the last stages of labour. Midwives were given the title 'servants of Heket' in honour of their life-giving work. The colours of Heket are green and pink.

The Creation of Life

Heket was often imagined to be one of a number of gods and goddesses who created the form of the unborn child in the womb. Some sources assumed her to be the female counterpart of the ram god Khnum who fashioned unborn children on his potter's wheel. It is not surprising that the frog became associated with gestation and childbirth. Adult frogs would have been plentiful at mating times and their eggs would have been abundant in the waters of the Nile and the Nile cataracts. As the Egyptians believed that life emerged from the primeval waters of Nu and that the Nile itself flowed from Nu, its water would have been indicative of new life, especially as it was essential to new crop growth and the nourishment of the Egyptian people and their livestock. The connection may have been strengthened by the observation of the foetal waters breaking prior to the birthing process. Children, like frogs, emerged from water.

Heket the Midwife

Once the unborn child had been formed in the womb and was ready to emerge into the world, it was Heket's job to preside over the birth. She was the divine midwife who protected the mother and baby during labour. It was thought that she could quicken the process of birth, particularly during the last stages, and could bring a degree of pain relief to the mother. Heket had the power to give life and she could facilitate an easier passage into the world for the new child.

Heket was a primitive goddess. Some accounts describe her as a daughter of Re and say that she was born from his mouth alongside the air god Shu. With other deities, she is thought to be one of the midwives who preside over the birth of the sun each morning.

Heket was the patron of mortal midwives and many of the women who fulfilled this important role were thought to be in service to her. Some had the name or the symbology of the frog goddess carved upon the paraphernalia that they carried with them.

The Symbology of the Frog

The image of Heket became a powerful totem of protection. Pregnant women in ancient Egypt often wore amulets or scarabs that bore depictions of frogs. These connected them with the sacred protection that this goddess could provide; helping them to place themselves in her custody during the period of gestation and birth. Heket was also a protector of the home. Magical knives bearing representations of the frog goddess were used during the Middle Kingdom to bring protection to the family unit.

Frogs are adaptable creatures who have succeeded in evolving to survive in many different environments throughout the world. In this respect they are similar to humankind. In Central American traditions the frog was thought to bring healing by cleansing negative energy and warding off evil. The protection of Heket, too, was there to dispel negative forces, allowing the safe passage of new life into the world.

HEKET IN A READING

Upright

If you have chosen this stone tablet in a reading then this is a time for enjoying the comfort, support and nourishment of your home life. It is important to concentrate on family concerns, close connections and intimacy, as well as the warmth and security that a good home can provide. If your home life is good then Heket urges you to celebrate that and encourages you to actively contribute to the harmony that you desire, whether you share your home with your parents, your partner, your lover, your children or your friends. If your home life leaves something to be desired then the influence of Heket can give birth to new impulses that will help you to heal old conflicts or step out and create a more nourishing environment for yourself. This is a good time to move house, undertake repairs, do some decorating or upgrade your home comforts.

On a higher level, you are given the opportunity to come home to yourself spiritually. It may be good to spend some time in quiet meditation, gentle contemplation and stillness. You may need to reduce your level of activity for a while so that you can give your energy and attention to the spiritual quickening that is occurring within you.

The stone of Heket augurs a period of expectancy and birth. If you are thinking of starting a family or having another child then this is a fortunate stone to choose. If, alternatively, you are giving birth to a new creative project then you are blessed with tender support and devoted loyalty from someone close to you. The good wishes of your intimate circle will help you to succeed. Remember to ask for their support when you need it and give thanks for all the love and care that you receive.

Reversed

If this stone tablet is reversed then you are the midwife of someone else's security, stability and renewed hope. Perhaps you are a wonderful homemaker who helps to create the special environment in which other people can be safe to live and thrive. The atmosphere that you establish around you, teamed with the physical comforts you provide, help to give the lives of others a sense of meaning and purpose. You furnish the people you love with a warm hearth and a warmer heart, and you are a central focus for their growth and development. People who are not yet part of your intimate circle also benefit from your compassion as you put them at their ease and help them to feel at home, even when you yourself are feeling vulnerable.

Alternatively, you may find yourself surrounded by expectant or broody parents who look to you for support and reassurance as they embark upon the creation of new life. You could soon discover that you have a new brother or sister, niece or nephew, godchild or grandchild. You may even become the midwife or godparent to a new creative endeavour that includes younger people.

This could involve you in promoting the rights and needs of children within your community. Memories of childhood may resurface and there are opportunities for healing your own inner child and for bringing comfort to the fears or childhood insecurities that others still carry within them.

Attributes

If this stone tablet represents a person then they will be both gentle and practical. She or he is very protective of other people and highly committed to creating the best for all concerned. This person could be a health professional or someone involved in childcare and education. They have a natural wisdom and often have good counselling skills or healing hands. They may also be a good homemaker. Their guidance of others is based upon their own hands-on experience and sound instincts. The qualities of Heket most directly relate to the signs of Cancer and Virgo in western astrology.

Meditation

Close your eyes, breathe deeply and relax. Ensure that your environment is warm and peaceful and curl up in a comfortable position. Imagine yourself, as you would have been, just prior to your birth and, in your mind, talk to the unborn baby you once were. Tell yourself it is safe to be alive and give your inner baby comfort and reassurance. Praise yourself and acknowledge as many of your positive qualities as you can. Give your inner baby the gift of the qualities you would like to develop in your life from now on: greater health, strength, wisdom or beauty perhaps, or a multitude of other attributes and talents. Picture yourself as an adult, growing into those qualities and displaying them with ease. Visualize your inner baby being born anew: peacefully, comfortably and with all the protection needed. The spirit of Heket guides your rebirth and welcomes you safely into the world. Take time to complete this meditation.

POSITIVE AFFIRMATIONS

I am my own healer and counsellor.
My intuition grows and develops every day.
I give birth to new ideas and fresh inspirations.
I trust my instincts to guide me towards my greatest happiness.
I easily quicken my spiritual growth and development.
It is safe for me to bring new things into the world.
I am adaptable and strong.

APIS

Bull God

— Power —

— Proclamation —

— Messages —

— Protection —

The god Apis was a living deity. He was represented by a series of living bulls, each of which were specially chosen from the herd and decorated for ceremonial purposes. Apis was thought to be a manifestation of the creator god Ptah and was worshipped as the energy of creation. He was often called the son of Ptah and was seen to be his herald or messenger. Apis is frequently depicted with a sun disk or moon disk resting between his horns and bearing the 'Uraeus', the cobra emblem of royalty. Often Apis is shown with the wings of the vulture goddess placed protectively across his back. The hairs of his tail are split and braided into two, perhaps representing the dual kingdom of Upper and Lower Egypt. His colour is violet.

The Sacred Messenger

Apis was originally a symbol of fertility and later became associated with the god Ptah. Both deities had their cult centre at Memphis, the political capital of ancient Egypt. Ptah, the creator god, was said to have fashioned other gods and all life. His priests maintained that he had even created Atum, the creator god of Heliopolis. Apis was thought to be a living manifestation of Ptah, or a herald and intermediary between the god and his mortal worshippers. In essence, the Apis bull was a physical form of the divine energy of creation; he provided Egyptians with a focus for their worship.

Over time, Apis developed additional qualities and associations. He became linked to Osiris and evolved into a mortuary god. On death, an Apis bull was thought to be absorbed into the personality of Osiris, becoming the combined deity Osiris-Apis. Curiously, though, it is Isis, wife and sister of Osiris, who is most commonly attributed with being the mother of the sacred bull.

The Life of an Apis Bull

The living Apis bull was selected from the herd because of his markings and characteristics. Apis was thought to have been conceived through a flash of lightning, and the Apis bull was always completely black except for a flash of white on his forehead in the shape of a triangle, and another shaped like a crescent moon on his side. His role was a ceremonial one, making special appearances at the festivals of Memphis and receiving the kind of attention normally devoted to royalty. On average, an Apis bull would live for fourteen years and his death would also be a ceremonial event with state mourning and ritualistic mummification. Apis bulls were buried, adorned with jewels, in specially cut tombs at the desert necropolis that overlooked Memphis.

Rather than through a flash of lightning, Apis is sometimes said to have been conceived by Ptah taking the form of a celestial fire and impregnating a virgin heifer. The black bull calf born from this union was said to be a reincarnation of Ptah himself, and was recognizable to the priests of Memphis by the mystic mark of a scarab beetle on its tongue, in addition to the previously mentioned flashes of white. The image of a scarab served to link Apis with the sun god.

The movements and behaviour of an Apis bull were looked on as having great religious and spiritual significance. Often his actions were interpreted as omens. Even his interest in an offering of food was thought to indicate future life and well-being while ardent disinterest could foretell an untimely death.

Sacred Bulls of Egypt

Apis is the best known of the sacred bulls of Egypt, but the worship of bulls was certainly present at more than one cult centre, and gods other than Ptah had bulls associated with them. At Heliopolis the bull sacred to Re-Atum was called Merwer or Mnevis. In a similar fashion to Apis, Merwer was imagined to be a messenger for his principal deity, the sun god.

APIS IN A READING

Upright

If you have chosen this stone tablet in a reading then the world is presenting you with messages of power. Everything you do, see and experience is encouraging you to recognize the power within yourself and is teaching you how to use it for the benefit of all concerned. This is not an abstract concept of power; rather it is the ability to harness your energy in a tangible way. Your power can have a practical, physical impact on the world around you, and events that are occurring now provide you with the opportunity to use it. This is power made manifest; it can alter the course of your life for the better and help you to establish your special gifts and talents. Harnessing this divine potential will create a period of physical progress and material success. Take pleasure in the sensuality of life.

The stone of Apis augurs a time when we can let go of the beliefs, habits and behaviour patterns that inhibit our potential. Some of us fear power because we have seen it abused on national and international levels, as well as in the family unit or the work place. However, this is not true power: it is a manipulation of authority and position. True power comes to us when our body, mind and emotions are properly aligned with our spiritual essence. It is the correct use of our life force that occurs when we are fulfilling our spiritual purpose and have come to a new understanding of our place within the greater scheme of things.

Perhaps the other reason we may fear power is that so many of us have learned, from childhood, to see ourselves as small and powerless. Becoming powerful may feel like stepping into unknown territory. Giving up beliefs and habits that limit our power allows us to make extraordinary changes. Negative thoughts, addictions to nicotine, alcohol, other recreational drugs and excessive eating, all dull our senses and disconnect us from our true nature. By changing these habits we grow in strength and grace.

Reversed

If this stone tablet is reversed then it is a time to recognize the spiritual essence in others and, in doing so, reconnect to the spiritual essence in yourself. When we remove prejudices and judgemental thoughts from our minds, we begin to see the true beauty behind the masks, affectations, behaviour and perceived faults of others. If we look carefully beneath the outward appearance that others present and listen attentively to them, we can make extraordinary discoveries. It is the messages that underpin the words that are uttered, rather than the words themselves, that are important.

When we see others for whom they truly are, then it allows us to let go of deeply ingrained fears and strengthen our trust in life. Practise seeing everyone you meet as an individual spark of divine creation and tell yourself that they are doing their best to follow their human path with the knowledge and awareness that is currently available to them. It may be a challenge to begin with but it will get easier. By seeing ourselves in a similar way, we can drop our feelings of inadequacy and dissolve the negative beliefs that perpetuate a lack of self-worth.

Attributes

If this stone tablet represents a person then he or she will be amiable, easy-going and generally accepting of others. They may have a message for you from another person, or their presence and behaviour may provide you with a message that will enhance your personal evolution. They may even carry messages of your achievements and positive qualities to others so that your reputation precedes you. This is an individual who is strong, physically and emotionally. They provide the people around them with safety, stability and a sense of security. The qualities of Apis most directly relate to the sign of Taurus in western astrology.

Meditation

Close your eyes, breathe deeply and relax. Picture an image of your body exactly as it is now. See the position of your arms, legs, head and spine. Then, picture another image of your body superimposed over the first; your position is exactly the same as in the original but the area that it covers is larger. Together they create the double-image of a body inside a body. The smaller one represents your physical frame; the larger one is your unique spiritual power.

Imagine your physical body expanding to encompass the divine purpose, higher awareness and positive, creative potential that is contained within your spiritual body; growing bigger until both images combine and then returning to its normal size. Visualize yourself going about your daily life, able to access and use your personal power during every thought, feeling and activity. Your power makes a positive difference to the world around you.

POSITIVE AFFIRMATIONS

I allow myself to grow into my power.
I view everyone with love, acceptance and compassion.
I easily see the divine spark within all life.
I easily see the divine spark within myself.
I use my power to make a positive, practical difference.
My world is filled with positive messages.
I am safe with my power.

MERETSEGER

Lover of Silence

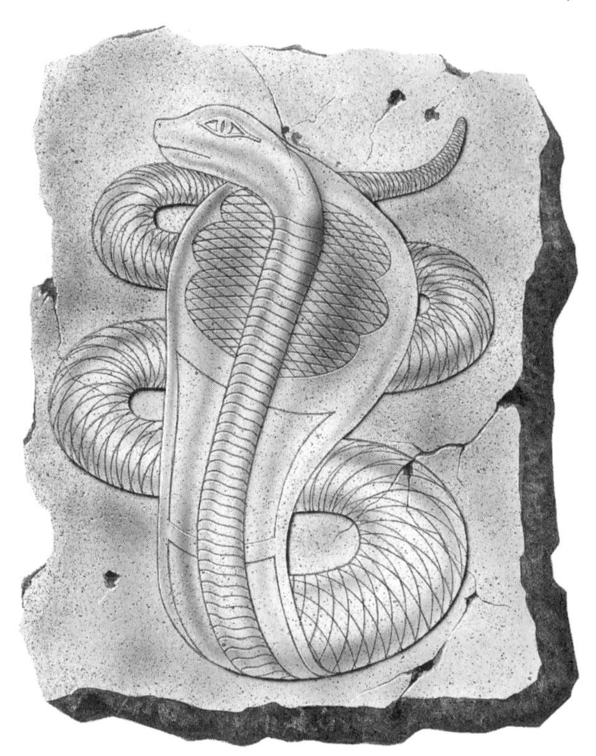

— Mercy —

— Honesty —

— Respect —

— Seclusion —

The goddess Meretseger is the cobra goddess who is said to dwell on the mountain that overlooks the Valley of the Kings. She is often depicted as a coiled snake or as a snake with a human head and an arm extending from her hood. Alternatively, she is sometimes seen as a female-headed scorpion. The translation of her name, Meretseger, is 'she who loves silence' or 'beloved of him (Osiris) who makes silence' and indeed she was often endowed with the guardianship of secluded tombs. Meretseger is both merciful and potentially dangerous; she is said to bring healing to those who are honest and respectful, and retribution to those who are not. The colour associated with the cobra goddess is dark green.

Goddess of the Peak

Near the Valley of the Kings there is a mountain that is known as 'Lady of the Peak'. This district of western Thebes is the domain of Meretseger who was the protecting deity of the area. The cobra goddess was imagined to dwell on the mountain, but her influence spread to cover the whole Theban necropolis area during the New Kingdom.

Meretseger was thought to guard secluded royal tombs. She was a silent presence who could blight wrongdoers with poison and physical afflictions, yet remain benign and merciful to those who approached with an honest heart. Her vengeance could kill but her mercy could bring miraculous healing. She was particularly worshipped by necropolis workers who both honoured and feared her. It was thought that workers who committed crimes would be struck down with venomous stings or afflicted with a loss of sight. However, even wrongdoers could be recipients of her mercy if they repented.

The Uraeus of Egypt

The cobra became a symbol of sovereignty in ancient Egypt. The cobra emblem, or 'Uraeus', appears again and again on the crowns and headdresses of royal figures. It was worn by Horus and Seth and was linked to the sun god Re. The cobra appeared, hood raised, poised to strike in defence of her monarch. It was thought that the Uraeus spat flames; her fire was the kiss of death to the king's enemies. Rather than having any direct connection to Meretseger, the Uraeus is associated with another cobra goddess, Wadjet. Wadjet was the cobra goddess of Buto in the northern Nile delta. She was thought to maintain the influence of royal authority in the north and it is perhaps for this reason that the Uraeus was often representative of Lower Egypt within royal symbolism. Some stories tell of her taking the form of a vengeful lioness with attributes that are similar to the lioness Sakhmet.

The Universal Power of the Snake

The snake is an animal that has attained mystical significance throughout the world. Snakes have been both feared and honoured, from the serpent in the Garden of Eden to the snake that is the emblem of the sixth year in the Chinese astrological cycle. Indeed, in China, snakes were considered to be lucky and people born within the year of the snake were thought to be attractive, sensual and seductive. Many cultures have associated snakes with the cycle of death and rebirth. The snake sheds its skin and emerges from the debris with a fresh skin and an appearance of renewed vitality.

Snakes have often been associated with the element of fire. They are the fire of new life that clears away the old and makes way for the new in a continuous cycle of transformation. Indian yogic traditions link snakes with the raising of the *Kundalini*, the life force energy that is thought to flow from the base of the human spine upwards. The snake was also part of the emblem of Asclepius, a Greek and Roman deity associated with medicine.

MERETSEGER IN A READING

Upright

If you have chosen this stone tablet in a reading then now is the time to take stock of your life and examine your motives before progressing further. It is important that the choices you make come from a position of respect for yourself and other people. If you are sure that you are operating from an honest heart, and you are willing to value yourself rather than allow yourself to be dishonoured or exploited, then it is time to proceed; but it is always worth stopping first and taking a few moments of silence to think things through. Similarly, if your actions or intentions dishonour another and do not come from respect and acceptance, stop now, think carefully and change your approach before proceeding. A willingness to act with honesty and integrity is often enough to divert your forward path and alter the progression of events so that your benefits increase and your tensions diminish.

The stone of Meretseger augurs a time of divine intervention. Plans may alter abruptly and there could be delays, but, before you become frustrated, be aware that what is occurring is beneficial for you. If a project has fallen through, let it go, and take time to listen to your intuitive, inner voice. Projects may be cleared from your path or delayed so that you can rethink your involvement and reinvent your future progress. They will either be replaced by something more appropriate to your needs or they will evolve into something more innovative than you had previously imagined. Similarly with relationships, taking time to think will bring unexpected benefits, improving communication and mutual understanding.

There is power in silence. So often we fill our lives with noise and activity, drowning out the inner voices and underlying feelings that could otherwise heal us. Do not fear silence; it brings love, reassurance and friendship to those who are willing to listen.

Reversed

If this stone tablet is reversed then you are being asked to exercise compassion, mercy and forgiveness. Judging others harshly and condemning them for their actions will not serve you. You will only clutter your mind with recriminating thoughts and impede your progress if you hold on to resentments or perpetuate a state of misunderstanding. When we are forgiving, we release ourselves from entrapments and create the freedom from old patterns of belief and behaviour that will allow us to develop healthier relationships. Forgiveness is a sign of strength and not a demonstration of weakness. When we forgive, we do not have to allow ourselves to be abused or dishonoured again. We have a right to put up clear boundaries and say no to relationships that are not healthy for us. The process of forgiveness is an essential part of moving on to better experiences.

Be forgiving and merciful now and the rewards will be numerous. You will become more available for the compassion and forgiveness in others when you are in your hour of greatest need. You will also become magnetic for relationships that are built on greater respect and integrity and you will benefit from clarity and peace of mind.

Attributes

If this stone tablet represents a person in your life then she or he will be generally tolerant and forgiving. They will be compassionate when dealing with the mistakes and failings of others but they do have clear boundaries and they demand honesty and respect from close associates. If treated unjustly or if their good nature is abused then their disapproval can be stinging, but beneath this they are a model of kindness. This person has a quiet intensity; they are subtle and seductive, and are able to penetrate your defences and probe into your inner feelings with very little effort. The qualities of Meretseger most directly relate to the sign of Scorpio in western astrology.

Meditation

Close your eyes, breathe deeply and relax. Picture yourself walking up the side of a mountain. The incline is steep but your path snakes back and forth, allowing you to climb quickly while maintaining a steady pace. As you ascend, your mind becomes clearer and any concerns drop away from you. See yourself reaching the peak, the domain of Meretseger, and imagine yourself to be protected by the mercy and compassion of this goddess. Picture yourself looking down over your life, gaining a clear vantage point over your current situation. You have a greater, more balanced perspective of your relationships, your health, your career and your spiritual development. From this vantage point, ask yourself the following questions and act on your instinctive answers: *'What is the most forgiving thing that I can do, think or say at this time?' 'How can I move forward in my life with greater honesty, respect and integrity?'*

POSITIVE AFFIRMATIONS

I easily forgive myself and others.
I am safe with stillness and silence.
It is easy for me to listen to my wise inner voice.
I give and receive respect wherever I go.
Truth protects me, forgiveness heals me.
It is safe for me to be honest.
I rethink my intention and reshape my future.

IMHOTEP

Sacred Scribe and Architect

— Administration —

— Instruction —

— Skill —

— Deification —

Imhotep was a living, historical figure who served as a high courtier under King Djoser in the third dynasty. He held the offices of chief executive and master sculptor. His creative and administrative talents were many; he is credited with the invention of building with cut stone and as the author of a book of instruction. It is also possible that he was the architect of the step pyramid at Saqqara. He is often depicted sitting with an open papyrus roll across his lap, and the papyrus roll is his symbol on the stone. Deification was a rare honour for a subject of the Pharaohs, and after his immortalization, Imhotep became the embodiment of scribal wisdom and a god of creative, scientific and architectural skill. His colours are oranges and yellows.

From Man to God

In ancient Egypt it was rare for a mortal man to be elevated to the ranks of the immortals unless, of course, he was of royal blood. The role of Pharaoh was an immortal one but normally the holder of any lesser role than this, however important, could not expect to join the ranks of the gods. He or she would have to be content with a degree of worldly recognition, fame and, perhaps, a reputation that lived on after his or her death.

Imhotep was one of the few, high-ranking, Egyptian officials whose impact upon Egyptian culture was considered significant enough for his successors to raise him to the level of a god. Another deified mortal was Amenhotep, son of Hapu, who was a minister of Amenhotep the third. Like Imhotep, he was a scribe and a builder who was often depicted in the seated scribal position and holding a roll of papyrus. However, unlike Imhotep, he only attracted a minimum amount of worship and did not attain the same level of divinity.

A God of Civilization

Imhotep was a deity who embodied many of the new skills and qualities of civilization. As an architect and builder he can be viewed as representative of the building blocks of the civilized world. Egypt was, after all, the first great nation state. It evolved from a collection of regions or 'nomes' into the dual kingdom of Upper and Lower Egypt. Imhotep held an additional role as a peacemaker, which is also indicative of civilization; it displays a trend towards peaceful coexistence that has continued to develop to the present day. Despite a level of continuing conflict in the world, many of its peoples have developed the diplomacy and tolerance to coexist as part of a global village.

Imhotep also embodied the skills of language and technology that have evolved into the global communication systems we have today. He was a patron of scribes and he protected anyone who was involved with the sciences and with occult practices. He was often depicted with the shaven head of a priest and was the patron of doctors. This suggests that the origins of medical science and spiritual healing may be one and the same. The knowledge and multitudinous skills of Imhotep may have been available to an educated elite in ancient times but their modern equivalents are now available to millions around the world.

The Triad of Memphis

Imhotep was adopted into the 'Triad of Memphis' as the son of Ptah and Sakhmet *(see pages 9–10)*. His adoption displaced the god Nefertum as the third member of this divine family. The creator god Ptah made an obvious 'father' for Imhotep. They were both gods of masonry and architecture. In later times, the worship of Imhotep appears to have eclipsed the attention given to Ptah himself. It is clear that, as a deity, rather than a historical figure, Imhotep grew to embody many of the same qualities as the great creator god of Memphis.

IMHOTEP IN A READING

Upright

If you have chosen this stone tablet in a reading then this is a time for sharpening your skills and becoming the efficient executive of your life and affairs. Progress can be made by developing and honing your craft, organizing your time more effectively or catching up with your administration. If you are ambitious, or have aspirations yet to be fulfilled, then your best course of action is to apply yourself and learn how to do your job as thoroughly and efficiently as you can. What do you need to learn in order to make your dreams become a reality? How can you organize your life more effectively so that you can achieve the most success or fulfilment with the minimum of effort?

Imhotep brings success in career and material advancement as well as in the development of higher reason and intellect. Choosing this stone can indicate that it is time to look for a new job, seek promotion or expand your brief. Your ability to take the initiative and be innovative in an ordered and effective manner has grown, and your responsibilities need to grow too so that you are properly stimulated. On the home front, this is an excellent time for rebuilding your life, moving house or renovating your existing property.

The stone of Imhotep augurs a time when you will feel peaceful within yourself and will create peacefulness around you. You may become involved with a project that will promote communication and understanding within your local community, your family circle or the world at large. You help to build bridges between individuals or organizations and create foundations for growth, change and development that will benefit others, even after you have moved on.

Reversed

If this stone tablet is reversed then you may find that someone else has become the architect of your happiness or affairs. Perhaps a friend, partner or colleague is providing you with effective administration that enables you to immerse yourself in the creative activities that you enjoy. They may furnish you with the organization, representation or structure that allows you to shine. It is also possible that someone is working behind the scenes to heal your relationships; creating peace between you and another party or arranging a new contact for you that will prove to be mutually beneficial.

Alternatively you may be achieving your ambitions or developing spiritually by aligning yourself with the progress of another. Perhaps the expertise of a partner, a lover, a child or a colleague is creating a new level of prosperity or influence that you are benefiting from. You may find yourself assuming a supportive role as someone close to you develops her or his career, or takes time out to train in a new skill. Their development brings you a level of advancement too and your devoted service brings you spiritual rewards. Just be sure that you do not lose your own sense of purpose or identity as you contribute to this person. Serving others can enhance your spiritual growth, but living your life through another individual could ultimately inhibit your development.

Attributes

If this stone tablet represents a person in your life then they will be an organizer, a diplomat and a technical or creative genius. He or she creates a sense of order wherever they go but it is order that is liberating rather than restrictive. Indeed, this person is so secure in his or her sense of order that they are willing to turn it upside down and break all the rules when they realize that their system or approach is beginning to inhibit the creative process. They know that they can always create a new order for themselves that will prove to be more effective than the one before. In western astrology, the qualities of Imhotep most directly relate to the signs of Taurus, Libra and Aquarius.

Meditation

Close your eyes, breathe deeply and relax. Visualize yourself with a magical book of instruction that has been created especially for you. It is beautifully bound and feels good to hold. Inside this book is all of the wisdom and guidance that you will ever need to make your life a success. It is filled with ideas to help you develop new skills, harness your talents and awaken your powers of invention. Each page holds a key to unlocking your special qualities.

Picture yourself opening your book at random and, in doing so, imagine that you reveal the perfect information for your creative or spiritual progress at this time. It could be a thought to ponder, a practical suggestion or words of reassurance. Listen for any thoughts that come into your mind and be aware of any feelings that touch your heart. With practice, this visualization can stimulate your unique, inventive genius. Act on any inspirations that you receive.

POSITIVE AFFIRMATIONS

I unlock my powers of invention.
I am free to construct the life that I choose.
I am the architect of my happiness and success.
I create peace, order and brilliance in my life and affairs.
I am protected and supported in all of my endeavours.
New knowledge and awareness is revealed to me.
It is easy for me to develop new skills.

THE PYRAMIDS

Structures of Power

— Group Consciousness —

— Geometry —

— Symbolism —

— Wonder —

The pyramids of ancient Egypt continue to inspire the world with awe and wonder. Many mysteries still surround them, from the exact interpretation of their purpose, to the marvel of their construction. The technology of pyramid design, their precise engineering and the manner in which their building materials were manoeuvred continues to baffle many experts. One thing is certain: the pyramids were the collective achievement of the gods and Pharaohs who inspired them, the architects who designed them and the vast workforce of stone masons and labourers who constructed them. It could be said that they are a monument to the collective genius of ancient-Egyptian culture.

The Pyramids at Giza

Perhaps the most famous of Egyptian pyramids are the three pyramids at Giza that stand upon a plateau on the western bank of the Nile near al-Jiza. They are listed amongst the seven wonders of the ancient world, alongside a collection of architectural achievements that includes the Colossus of Rhodes, the Hanging Gardens of Babylon and the Pharos Lighthouse of Alexandria. Although these pyramids pre-date the other 'wonders', their construction has proved to be the most effective at withstanding the passage of time.

Of the three pyramids, the oldest is the Great Pyramid which is thought to have been built by Khufu, the second king of the fourth dynasty. However, there have been speculations that suggest this structure could be older than is currently believed and that it could be a monument to a sophisticated society that pre-dates the Egyptians. The existence of such a race is conjecture, but it is imagined that they were in command of technologies that surpass much of what we have developed today.

The second pyramid is commonly attributed to King Khafre of the fourth dynasty, who is also linked to the construction of the Great Sphinx nearby. The final and most southerly of the three pyramids is attributed to King Menkaure, the sixth monarch of this dynasty. The three pyramids are accompanied by smaller ones built as tombs for members of the royal family, and flat-topped 'mastabas' constructed for the burials of other relatives and court officials.

Preserving Powers

Research into the shape and structure of pyramids has brought some interesting results. The space inside a pyramid is thought to have properties that slow down the natural process of decay. This effect must have proved particularly beneficial to a culture that placed great emphasis on preserving the bodies of dead Pharaohs for rebirth in the afterlife. Experiments with small pyramids have indicated that they do indeed have an effect on the rate of decay for fruit and vegetables, as well as preserving the cutting edge of sharp knives. The reason for this is unclear, but some sources postulate that the pyramids are an example of a lost science of geometric engineering that is able to affect the nature of time itself.

The Magical Qualities of the Pyramid

In addition to the preserving powers of the pyramids, mystics and spiritual masters have also reported that pyramids can help to facilitate a change in consciousness when used in sacred ceremonies, meditation and shamanic rites of passage. They are reputed to provide doorways to a state of timelessness that allows the human mind access to the realms beyond linear thought and awareness. However, it is also suggested that it takes a person with spiritual maturity and great stability to handle this kind of universal vision; our minds have yet to evolve the capacity to process the scale of information pyramids can promote.

THE PYRAMIDS IN A READING

Upright

If you have chosen this stone tablet in a reading then this is a time for awakening knowledge and awareness from within. Your inner geometry or energetic structure is pre-programmed with knowledge and awareness; this has surfaced to shape your life and destiny now. Contained within the cells of your body is the knowledge of your ancestors, the matrix of your spiritual self and the programme of your divine purpose. If you hold a belief in reincarnation you may wish to consider that your other lives or other states of existence are having a direct influence on the events, feelings and experiences you are passing through now. Ask yourself for instinctive information about your spiritual origins and about your ultimate spiritual direction. You may gain some interesting insights. Are you from the Earth and looking up at the stars or are you from the stars and choosing to walk upon the Earth? The clues to your true identity come from within.

The stone tablet of The Pyramids augurs a period of extraordinary self-realization when you are able to remember a little more of your true nature and harness abilities that you had forgotten or that you did not even know you had. This may come with a flash of inspiration or a sudden realization of something that you have known all along but have only now been able to formulate as thoughts, words or tangible feelings. It may also come with a momentary sense of timelessness and wonder; a glimpse beyond the veil of linear time to reveal a little more of the true nature of the universe. Time, as we interpret it, where everything that happens appears to occur in a simple logical sequence, is an illusion. True time travel is something that can take place within the human consciousness once we have developed the strength, wisdom and stability to handle this aspect of our evolution.

Reversed

If this stone tablet is reversed then you are being reminded that your personal development is linked to the group mind or collective consciousness. Just as we have our individual minds and our own higher consciousness that directs our path towards growth and enlightenment, we are also part of a group mind that facilitates the evolution of humankind. The principles of development and civilization were thought waves that passed through the collective consciousness before manifesting in the physical world and changing the way that we live. The impulses to invent new technologies, philosophies and moral codes all began as a series of thoughts in the group mind.

To achieve the greatest happiness and success now, it is important that you work in harmony with the group mind. Miraculous changes and seemingly impossible tasks can be achieved with team work. New projects facilitate you working more closely with colleagues, family, friends or community groups than ever before. Solutions come when you ask for help and stay open to receive the advice and practical assistance that other people have to offer you. You develop the greatest personal satisfaction at this time by putting the needs and goals of the group first. Concentrate on creating a win for everyone and not just for yourself.

Attributes

If this stone tablet represents a person who has come into your life then she or he will remind you of your spiritual origins and destiny. Perhaps this is a person who has come from the same spiritual family as yourself. They have a similar purpose to yours and you share a relationship with them that is both mutually understood and impossible to put into words. Our true spiritual family is not necessarily the same as our genetic family but the two can sometimes overlap. This person could be a friend or relative in spirit who is still there to guide you even though you are not physically related.

Meditation

Close your eyes, breathe deeply and relax. Imagine that each cell of your body is made up of beautiful geometric patterns and you are able to look at an individual cell under a special powerful microscope. Picture a whole universe of patterns and shapes that are exquisite to behold. Visualize spirals of light travelling in all directions through this geometric universe and wherever they move, see the shapes begin to modify and change.

Imagine the light gently and effectively transforming the structure within each cell so that your spiritual purpose is highlighted and enhanced. See your cells re-creating themselves in health, vitality and joy as the light programs them for happiness, prosperity, well-being and success. Your cellular structure becomes magnetic to the fulfilment of your goals, and you become magnetic to your true, spiritual family. People who remind you of your spiritual origins and highest potential are drawn to you.

POSITIVE AFFIRMATIONS

I easily regain my sense of wonder.
I draw new ideas and fresh inspiration from the group mind.
The shape and structure of my life supports my happiness.
I receive the grace and guidance of my spiritual ancestors.
My life is part of a greater plan.
My spiritual origins are now revealed to me.
I surrender to my higher purpose.

THE SPHINX

The Sands of Time

— Secrets —

— Enigma —

— Longevity —

— Patience —

The Sphinx gazes out over the sands of time; a composite creature with the body of a lion and, in most cases, a human head. There were many sphinxes in the ancient world but the most famous is the Great Sphinx at Giza which is thought to date from the reign of Khafre, the fourth king of the fourth dynasty. However, there are some who believe that the Great Sphinx and the first Great Pyramid of Giza are actually much older than is generally accepted, built by a highly evolved people from a forgotten time. Whether it was built by the ancient Egyptians or by an extraordinary civilization that pre-dates them, it is clear that the Great Sphinx has witnessed numerous changes and is the guardian of many secrets.

The Egyptian Sphinx

Many Egyptian sphinxes are thought to carry the facial likeness of royal figures. Most are male, although there are a few Egyptian sphinxes that are female. Unlike the sphinx of Greek mythology who was clearly feminine and feared as a force of vengeance and destruction, the sphinx of Egypt was considered to be a benevolent influence on all except the enemies of the Pharaoh. Whatever else the sphinx may have represented, it is fairly clear that it was a symbol of royal power and guardianship. Sphinxes were often depicted in battle, casting down the foes of Egypt and trampling down any resistance to royal campaigns. However, the full meaning and purpose of the sphinx can only be guessed at; it would appear that the great composite beast of ancient Egypt has secrets that it will hold on to for a very long time to come.

A number of temples had avenues of sphinxes guarding their approach. At Karnak, ram-headed sphinxes were created in honour of the god Amun. Sphinx imagery was also popular within jewellery design and sphinxes were carved on scarabs and other ceremonial items.

The Construction of the Great Sphinx

The Great Sphinx at Giza is considered to represent Harmachis, the god of the rising sun, whose name is understood to mean 'Horus of the Horizon'. It is generally thought that it was built by King Khafre and that it was part of his funerary complex. The features of the Great Sphinx are believed to be a portrait of Khafre. The Sphinx appears to have been sculpted from an outcrop of limestone and is approximately two hundred and forty feet long and sixty-six feet high.

It is believed that when the Great Sphinx was constructed, the surrounding area was quite different from the desert landscape that is there today. It is thought that the Sphinx was surrounded by lush vegetation and may have been geographically close to an expanse of water much larger than the Nile, possibly even a stretch of ocean. Today's desert terrain may have been the outcome of major global changes. These could have resulted from a shift of the Earth's axis with a subsequent movement of land masses and dramatic changes of climate within most areas of the world, including the land of Egypt.

The Restoration of the Great Sphinx

Between the paws of the Great Sphinx is a stela with an inscription recording its partial renovation by Tuthmosis the fourth. The then prince, Tuthmosis was in the area on a hunting expedition. Growing tired, he fell asleep in the shadow of the Sphinx, who then appeared to the prince in a dream, promising him the throne of Egypt in return for clearing away the sand that buried and almost completely obscured the Sphinx's body. Tuthmosis did as he was asked and was rewarded with a reign of eight years from 1425 to 1417 BC.

THE SPHINX IN A READING

Upright

If you have chosen this stone tablet in a reading then this is a time for patience and trust. Nothing that is truly valuable is ever lost and no spiritual reward is ever denied you, so let go of any struggle and trust that what is rightfully yours will come your way at the right time. If you have easily adopted a patient state of grace then you are to be congratulated, you are exercising a level of wisdom and maturity that comes with an inner knowing that you are safe in the world.

If patience eludes you, then now is the time to let go of any desperation, obsessive activity or fear of lack, because the sands of time are shifting at their own pace and not at yours. Let go and trust; the rewards will be delicious if you allow them to arrive in their own time and in their own way. Ask for what you desire but do not attempt to control the manner in which the fulfilment of your desires will be provided for you. Affirm for everything you need but allow the universe to deliver your requests in ways that are aligned with your highest good.

The stone tablet of The Sphinx augurs a period when delicious secrets surround you and the mysteries of the universe thrill and inspire you. Do not dampen your curiosity but learn to be at peace with the fact that you do not always benefit from knowing everything at once. Being curious is generally healthy but needing to know the answer to all of life's mysteries, because of a desperation to stay in control, is not. Do your best to take charge of your life but if you find that you become desperate to control the outcome of every project, relationship or event, then discipline yourself to take two steps backwards. Patience is the lesson and faith, trust and imagination are the solutions. You cannot find the answers outside of yourself; it is time to develop a stronger sense of security within.

Reversed

If this stone tablet is reversed then you are the guardian of secrets for another. It is important that you keep what you know to yourself. Revealing information prematurely will not benefit you or anyone else. However, you will benefit from being a valued and trustworthy confidant, and your discretion will strengthen your relationships, bringing you greater intimacy or respect than ever before. Make sure that you act from diplomacy, tact and wisdom; the rewards will come to you in their due time.

Alternatively, you are the secret and your life is an enigma to others. You are viewed as mysterious and exotic, your motives are beyond the comprehension of others, and you become an object of curiosity. This is probably healthy and it would be best for you to keep your own counsel and not rush to dispel any myths. However, if your secrecy contributes to a state of misunderstanding then it may be wise to put a few people straight about your intentions. This does not mean you need to reveal all your business, but it does mean that you need to be honest about anything that may directly or indirectly affect others. It is possible that you will be a presence in their lives for a considerable time and, while it may benefit you to maintain an air of mystery, it would not benefit you to be constantly misinterpreted.

Attributes

If this stone tablet represents a person then she or he will either be long-lived or they will become a continual presence in your life over the months and years to come. This person could be a special confidant whom you learn to trust with your intimate secrets. They are willing to offer you wise counsel and to provide a listening ear; they are unlikely to repeat anything that you tell them. Alternatively, this is someone who entrusts you with important secrets of their own or who instructs you in the mysteries of the universe. The secrets they share could alter the course of your life for the better.

Meditation

Close your eyes, breathe deeply and relax. Imagine yourself living a long, healthy, fulfilling life and visualize yourself as elderly and yet youthful. See yourself still filled with vitality, joy and the capacity to take charge of your destiny. From this vantage point, imagine you are able to look back on your life to assess the wisdom and insights you received and the choices you made that contributed to your health and success.

Ask your future self to share his or her secrets with you. What information would most benefit you at this present time? What could you do now to ensure your longevity, health and happiness? What do you need to know to make the most of your life and enhance your spiritual evolution? Open your mind to any secrets that your future self wishes to share with you. They could come as thoughts, feelings, mental pictures, abstract concepts or gut impulses. Record these insights and act on them.

POSITIVE AFFIRMATIONS

My life is filled with rewards.
I am blessed with patience and grace.
I have all the time that I need for my desires to be fulfilled.
My secrets are honoured and respected.
I have faith, trust and imagination in abundance.
I am safe with the mystery of life.
I live a long and happy life.

PART THREE

CASTING FOR VISION AND CREATIVITY

'I am the Eye of Horus; I have opened the Eye of Horus in his hour.'
'O Eye of Horus support me ...'
THE EGYPTIAN BOOK OF THE DEAD

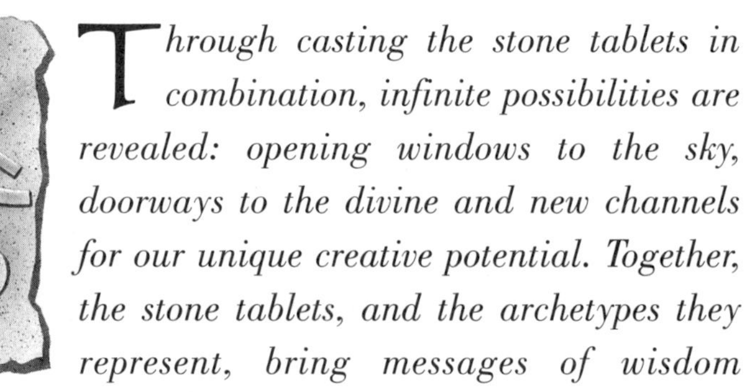

Through casting the stone tablets in combination, infinite possibilities are revealed: opening windows to the sky, doorways to the divine and new channels for our unique creative potential. Together, the stone tablets, and the archetypes they represent, bring messages of wisdom beyond their individual divinatory meanings. Here is a selection of original spreads for you to explore. They bring vision, creativity and divination. Mastery of the stones in combination brings with it an expansion of intuition and an awakening of inner wisdom. It is a resource that can grow with you as you grow, fly with you as you fly. Open The Eye of Horus, *look through it and allow its vision to support your wings as you take to the air ...*

HOW TO BEGIN

Within the introductory text of this book, I have discussed the regular practice of using one stone tablet at a time to bring clarity and inspiration for the day, week or month ahead, or in answer to a specific enquiry. This method of consulting stones is highly effective for general use, but from time to time you may wish to conduct a reading for yourself or for another person that goes into greater depth. Drawing a combination of stone tablets, unseen, to be read together, provides you with many more facets for contemplation. The relationship between two or more stones has a divinatory meaning that is greater than the individual meanings when read separately. Casting a spread of stone tablets can indicate a progression of the spiritual and creative trends likely to occur over a period of time, or demonstrates the different influences at work within a given situation or relationship.

I would now like to guide you through a number of original spreads, explaining their purpose and offering suggestions on how to practise them as effectively as possible. I have also included some sample readings to help you. These spreads will work beautifully, particularly if you become familiar with the stones and practise reading with them regularly. The key to conducting a good reading is to be so familiar with the material in this book that you can allow your intuition free rein. In doing so, you may discover that you know a great deal more about these sacred archetypes and how they relate to human nature than you realize.

Learning to Read the Stone Tablets

If you are wishing to read the stone tablets for other people it is a good idea to practise first. Use the stones individually on a daily basis as described in Part One and reread the divinatory meanings and background material regularly so you become familiar with the symbols and their interpretations. As you digest the material contained within this book, you will learn to go beyond it to develop your powers of intuition and your innate awareness of sacred archetypes.

When you begin to use the spreads it is best to cast and read each one for yourself, preferably a few times over, before turning your attention to reading for other people. The Eye of Horus spread is an exception to this, as it is generally intended to be cast only once for an individual. It is good to become familiar with the positions of the stone tablets and the rhythm or intention of each spread. The more you practise, the easier it will be for you to be creative in combining the individual meanings of the stones to produce something greater. You will discover that all the stones have their own relationships with each other and that new divinatory meanings can spring from every spread you read.

When you first start to do readings for other people, it is fine to have the book in front of you and to read out the divinatory meanings as written. Just make it clear to the person you are reading for that you are still learning and that you will be referring to the text throughout. It may be helpful to read out a passage, discuss it between you and then reread some key points or ideas before moving on. Using the text to stimulate an exchange of ideas between yourself and the seeker will bring clarity and illumination for you both. For the seeker, it will personalize the reading and help it to make sense. For you, it will teach you more about the stone tablets and how to interpret them in future readings.

As your confidence grows you will find yourself putting the book to one side and conducting a reading from memory, instinct and intuition. Even as they turn up again and again, the stone tablets will hold slightly different meanings for each individual seeker and for each specific question or situation they are cast for. Once you are comfortable with the basic interpretations, you can have more freedom to explore these subtle nuances. The stones, and the spiritual archetypes that they represent, have many more facets than can be written about in one book. Their power lies in the individual relationship that each reader develops with them and the doors that they can open within the human psyche.

Even when you become skilled at reading with the stones, it is often useful to go back to the book occasionally to revise the divinatory meanings. It is always valuable to have the book close at hand during readings in case you need to clarify certain points. Ultimately, the text is there to support you as you read the stones, but do not allow your use of it to inhibit your intuition and natural style as a stone-tablet reader. It is there to act as a springboard for your own instinctual knowledge and awareness. Learn to trust your intuition.

Where to do a Reading

For all readings it helps to create a 'sacred space': an atmosphere of peace and calm where you are able to use your intuition and greater awareness without distractions or clutter. Choose somewhere that is comfortable and quiet, unplug telephones and do your best to be away from anyone who is not actively involved in the reading, or who may be vying for your attention. If it suits you, it is often helpful to have soft lighting. Some people like to have music playing in the background but I find that this can be a distraction. If you do choose music, make sure that it is soft, peaceful and purely instrumental. Lyrics may create subliminal messages that affect your concentration or the concentration of the person you are reading for, or may distort the mood of the reading.

How Much Time to Allow

To read each spread properly you will need to allow plenty of time. Shorter spreads can take from twenty minutes to half an hour while the longer ones can take over fifty minutes, depending on whether you are reading for yourself or for someone else. Of course, the timing is ultimately dependent on you as a reader and the level of discussion or contemplation that you can stimulate. When you conduct a reading, take enough time to develop a level of depth and for ideas to be digested as fully as possible. However, be careful that neither you, nor the person you are reading for, gets tired, distracted or bored. When both parties are interested and fully involved in an extensive discussion, then a reading from the longest spread, the Eye of Horus spread, can take up to two hours.

Reading for Yourself

If you are doing a reading for yourself then you may choose to have a pen and paper or a tape recorder to make a record of the stones you cast and their positions. It is also useful to record your initial question or area of enquiry, if you have one, and any flashes of inspiration that you receive. Only involve another person in the reading if you truly trust their opinions and insights, and they are actively engaged in helping you to discuss and understand the ideas that emerge. Otherwise, act as your own guide and teacher in contemplating the stone tablets. Ask yourself to clarify each new idea by deciding what it means for you, how it feels and what it stimulates inside you. If it awakens memories, aspirations, new ideas, old fears or new understandings, acknowledge them to yourself and then record them for later use.

Reading for Someone Else

If you are reading for someone else, choose a location that, although safe, peaceful and comfortable for you both, is different from the places you choose for your rest and relaxation. Readings can facilitate powerful but gentle healing and personal development. You may wish to have somewhere to retreat to afterwards that is not cluttered by the ideas, feelings, needs or aspirations of the person you have been reading for. Your personal meditation space is there for you to recharge your physical, emotional, mental and intuitive batteries, and, as such, it needs to remain as clear as possible. A separate room is ideal but, if there is no other choice, use different areas within the same room for conducting readings and for your own recreation.

When reading for another person, it is best to have a pen and paper and a tape recorder. With the pen and paper you can record the positions of the stones for future use, and with the tape recorder you can record your reading and the dialogue between you. Of course, disregard this if the seeker does not wish to have a recording or does not feel comfortable with having any personal details stored in this way. I find, however, that most people want to have a tape to take away with them so they can use the material again.

Before You Begin

Casting a spread and conducting a reading can bring an extraordinary level of clarity, awareness and illumination to any area of enquiry that you, or the person seeking guidance, may have. The purpose of the stone tablets is to highlight the spiritual and creative influences that are having an effect upon individual personal development at the time of the enquiry. This includes past and future influences which are cast in relation to the dreams, needs, fears, expectations and aspirations of the seeker at the present moment. In consulting the stones, we, and those who seek our counsel, are able to better understand our underlying motives, to heal areas of internal conflict, and to make informed choices about our next steps forward. To ensure that the readings you conduct, whether for yourself or someone else, run as smoothly as possible, follow the advice and general guidelines laid out in this section.

Often the stone tablets are powerfully revealing; this is especially true when they are laid out in a spread. A reading can therefore be an intimate, or even quite vulnerable, experience. For this reason it is important that readings are conducted in an air of trust and confidentiality. The privacy and dignity of the seeker, the reader and anyone else involved, need to be fully honoured. Make an agreement of confidentiality at the beginning of each reading and stick to it. Only reveal the information that you and the seeker have shared during a reading to a third party if the seeker has given you clear permission to do so.

It is also important to make your readings as positively focused as possible. Planting negative expectations in the minds of others is unhelpful and potentially disruptive for them. The power of the self-fulfilling prophecy is very strong and people can think their way into problems that are neither necessary nor inevitable. The influences indicated by the stone tablets are there to be used constructively and are intended to stimulate positive thought and positive expectations of the future. A positive approach to life can bring about transformational solutions to even the most challenging situations. Negative or limiting expectations, on the other hand, serve no good purpose for anyone concerned.

When using *The Eye of Horus*, remember to respect the gods, goddesses and symbols that are associated with the stone tablets. Every stone represents a powerful archetype and may have powerful mental, emotional and spiritual influences. Before each reading, respectfully ask the stones for their help and regularly give thanks for their guidance and illumination.

As a reader, avoid imposing your ideas on other people and do not make important choices for them. Instead, try to provide those seeking your guidance with more background information to their situation and a space to examine and discuss the decisions that they wish to make. The reader's role is to support, clarify and advise and not to rob other people of their right to choose for themselves. It is through making our own choices that we may learn and grow in our lives.

Finally, whether reading for yourself or someone else, have as much fun as you can and trust your instincts. If you enjoy the process of reading then others are more likely to benefit from the readings you give. As you learn to trust yourself as a reader, you will make some extraordinary discoveries along the way.

CHOOSING THE RIGHT SPREAD

Here is a guide to the five original spreads that follow. Take some time at this stage to choose the one that is going to be the most appropriate for your needs or for the needs of the person you are reading for.

The Wisdom of Maat Spread

The Wisdom of Maat is a spread of three stones. It is designed to bring clarity and harmony to any choice you or the seeker needs to make. Use the Wisdom of Maat spread if:

- You (or the seeker) are confronted with a challenging decision and need help in making the right spiritual or moral choice.
- You (or the seeker) are faced with a conflict of interests within a particular relationship or with conflicting needs and impulses within yourself.
- You (or the seeker) have a specific need or enquiry to be addressed.
- The focus of enquiry is centred upon the dilemmas and choices of the present and immediate future.

The Secrets of the Sphinx Spread

The Secrets of the Sphinx spread is a cast of four stone tablets that represents a secret journey into the future. This is a spread that highlights our personal development over a passage of time, pointing out the lessons the future has to teach us. The four stones can be read as a progression of four days, four weeks, four months, four seasons or four years, as the seeker has chosen to be most appropriate for themselves. Use the Secrets of the Sphinx spread if:

- You (or the seeker) are particularly interested in the near future and the influences or life lessons that lie ahead for the period addressed in the reading.
- You (or the seeker) require a general reading of future trends.
- You (or the seeker) require general clarification of direction.

The Treasures of the Pyramids Spread

The Treasures of the Pyramids is a spread of five stones that gives the seeker an overview of a particular situation, allowing them to see a bigger picture of their life. The treasures it holds are representative of past, present and future in relation to a specific area of enquiry. Use the Treasures of the Pyramids spread if:

- You (or the seeker) wish to focus on the future trends within one specific area of life. This might be intimate relationships, family relationships, career development or spiritual awakenings.
- You have plenty of time. A period of at least forty-five minutes is required to contemplate or discuss all the facets of this enlightening spread.
- You are in an environment that is free from distractions and is conducive to a reading of greater depth.

The Relationship Spread

The Relationship spread is a cast of two stones that highlights the underlying forces or spiritual dynamics of any given relationship, be it with family, friends, a lover or a business partner. It can be referred to for relationships in the past, present or future. Use the Relationship spread if:
• You (or the seeker) wish to understand an unresolved relationship from the past.
• You (or the seeker) wish to bring healing and illumination to an ongoing relationship.
• You (or the seeker) wish to clarify the nature and potential of a new relationship.

The Eye of Horus Spread

The Eye of Horus is the most elaborate and the most universal of the five spreads described. It is a cast of seven stone tablets which acts as a personal totem of power, creativity and spiritual purpose. It is normally cast once only, but can be used many times as the basis for other readings and as an essential personal reference. Use the Eye of Horus spread if:
• You have plenty of time. At least an hour is needed to contemplate or discuss all of the facets of this spread and how it relates to your life or the life of the seeker.
• You (or the seeker) instinctively feel that it is the right time to clarify some fundamental life issues such as, *'Why am I here?'* or *'What is my spiritual purpose?'*
• You are in an environment that is free from distractions and is conducive to a reading of great depth.
• You have enough energy and concentration to complete the reading as thoroughly as possible.
• You (or the seeker) wish to create a blueprint that brings depth and clarity to other readings.

USING THE WISDOM OF MAAT SPREAD

The Wisdom of Maat spread is a cast of three stone tablets relating to moral choices, balance and justice. It empowers the seeker with the appropriate spiritual, emotional and mental approach to aid them with their decision making. Casting the stones in this way brings clarity, harmony and healing to the areas of internal and external conflict that are being addressed.

The Stone Tablets

Three stone tablets are chosen, unseen, from the bag. They are then placed in a line from left to right in front of the seeker as shown below, noting which stones were chosen upright and which reversed.

THE WISDOM OF MAAT SPREAD

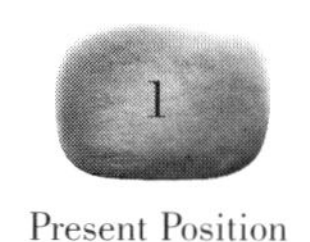

Present Position

Spiritual or Moral Choice

Path to Wisdom

1. PRESENT POSITION

This stone shows the seeker's present position: their hopes, fears, wishes and intentions.

2. SPIRITUAL OR MORAL CHOICE

The second stone highlights the spiritual or moral choice that the seeker is facing.

3. PATH TO WISDOM

The third stone brings the path to wisdom or the wisest course of action for the seeker.

SAMPLE READING

1. Present Position
Horus Reversed

2. Spiritual or Moral Choice
Nut Upright

3. Path to Wisdom
Anubis Upright

The subject of the reading is called Bill. He is contemplating a change of career; he has been an Arts Administrator for seven years, having trained in this field at college. He has worked his way up to a reasonably comfortable position with some ongoing security and a fair level of responsibility, but he is now feeling stuck and a little stagnant. His job does not offer any immediate hope of further promotion and he feels that he has neither the opportunity to make the kind of money he would like nor is he as satisfied creatively as he would hope to be. Bill is thirty; he is unsure whether to stay where he is for another couple of years or whether to get out now and train in some other field. He is interested in complementary therapies and public relations but has not, as yet, sought tangible ways of moving into either of these areas. His question is: *Would this be a good time for me to leave my job?*

The stone tablets are placed into the bag and Bill is asked to choose three of them, unseen, and place them in a line in front of him from left to right. It is noted which stone tablets have been drawn in their upright position and which have been drawn in a reversed position.

1. PRESENT POSITION

Horus Reversed

This shows Bill as someone who communicates information to others. This is borne out by the public relations and publicity aspects of his current position and the pleasure he derives from these areas of his work. The stone of Horus provides a reminder here that Bill would benefit from acknowledging and building upon these responsibilities, despite the other, more mundane aspects of his job that are getting him down.

It also shows him to be someone with a great deal of personal vision who is an inspiration to others. This may also indicate that he is building his personal vision of his future career at this time.

2. SPIRITUAL OR MORAL CHOICE

Nut Upright

Nut in this position could indicate a fear of stepping out into the unknown. Nut is the firmament that separates formlessness and chaos from all that is currently in existence. Her vastness and expanse would indicate that the issue here is not a lack of choices: there are limitless possibilities just waiting to be explored. It is this infinite variety of possibilities that is proving to be somewhat daunting for Bill.

A wise and intuitive reader of the stones may suggest that Bill would benefit from doing some research into the areas that interest him and begin to work out some tangible options. The sky is the limit and Bill is well supported in expanding his horizons at this time, but having more information would help him to feel more comfortable in taking the next step.

The presence of Nut does provide a degree of maternal protection and promises an abundance of opportunities or potential rewards to be recognized and claimed. The omens are good for any big decisions.

The combination of Horus and Nut in these positions emphasizes the expansiveness of the situation. Nut is the sky goddess and Horus is the lord of the skies, so it is certainly a time to think big, have a strong personal vision and step out into a wider arena.

3. PATH TO WISDOM

Anubis Upright

This is an excellent placing for Anubis. Bill is offered a great deal of protection if he chooses to move out into unknown territory and he will receive guidance through any unforeseen challenges or opportunities. Anubis also highlights the need to follow one's own intuition. Bill needs to look inside himself for answers rather than attempt to make logical sense of his situation. The message is to go with what you feel and trust the outcome.

An intuitive reader of the stone tablets may question Bill about his personal illusions, negative expectations and limited thinking. While the limitless possibilities indicated by the previous stones are certainly there, it is possible that Bill is limiting his way forward through a lack of self-belief or self-esteem. Anubis brings an energy that can help to shatter self-delusions of this kind and bring about a more positive, expansive view of self-worth and potential. If Bill's expectations of his future career are negative or restrictive then he would benefit from changing the way that he is thinking about his situation at this time.

The influence of Anubis does indicate that he has outgrown his current job and that it is time to move on to pastures new. Bill's interest in complementary therapies is also favourably indicated with Anubis, the bringer of healing powers, in this position.

The combination of Nut and Anubis indicates a need for humour and laughter. Taking a light-hearted approach will help Bill to take the next step.

Overview

The possibilities are good for moving out into something new. It is a time of personal development and growth where Bill's view of himself is expanding beyond his career expectations that became set in early adulthood. He could be encouraged to take the most expansive approach to his current job by asking himself what he could do to make it as creative and fulfilling for himself as possible, while at the same time taking tangible steps to move out in a new direction. He could help himself by:

- Doing more research. This could involve looking at job advertisements, finding out about courses that interest him and taking careers advice to find out where else his skills and training may be used.
- Thinking positively about himself, his skills and the opportunities available.
- Trusting his intuition and doing what he feels to be right for himself, rather than automatically taking the most logical or the safest option.
- Taking positive action sooner rather than later. Another two years in his current job would not serve him unless he used it to support himself through part-time training, or unless he managed to change the nature of his job to embrace more of his creative potential.

With the Wisdom of Maat spread, the stone tablet chosen in the third position is perhaps the most significant one. Bill may benefit from choosing to meditate on the stone of Anubis, using the visualizations or affirmations suggested. He could also keep a dream log to discover intuitive messages within his dreams.

USING THE SECRETS OF THE SPHINX SPREAD

The Secrets of the Sphinx is a four-stone spread and provides the seeker with a unique insight into the future. It shows an individual's development over a period of time. The four stones can be read as the four seasons, giving a progression for the year ahead or, alternatively, as four days, four weeks, four months or four years.

This spread gives an indication of the life lessons and influences available in the near future, based on the aspirations, mood and choices of the present. It provides a good general reading of the trends to come and helps clarify direction. However, as with any reading that focuses on the future, future trends read in the stones are not fixed in stone. We are free to act on the information we receive, making different choices that will alter these influences accordingly.

To begin this reading it is important to decide on the time frame of the enquiry and to stick to it. If you have decided to read for the next four days and the stones are chosen with this intention, then that is what the reading will reflect. If you then decide that a four-week reading would be more appropriate, it will require a reselection of stones.

The Stone Tablets

The four stones are chosen, unseen, from the bag and are then spread in an 'S' shape starting from the bottom as shown.

THE SECRETS OF THE SPHINX SPREAD

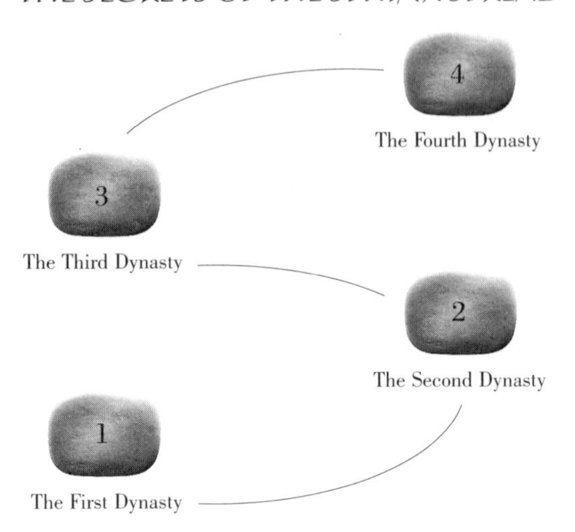

1. THE FIRST DYNASTY

The first stone represents the first period of enquiry. This could be the day, week, month, season or year ahead, as chosen.

2. THE SECOND DYNASTY

The second stone represents the second period of enquiry, highlighting the trends for the appropriate timescale.

3. THE THIRD DYNASTY

The third stone represents the third period of enquiry according to the reading's focus.

4. THE FOURTH DYNASTY

The fourth stone represents the last period of enquiry; the trends for the final day, week, month, season or year covered.

SAMPLE READING

4. The Fourth Dynasty
Bastet Upright

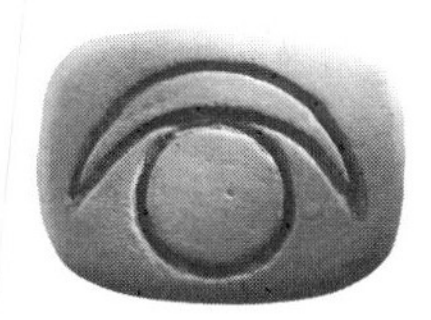

3. The Third Dynasty
Khonsu Reversed

2. The Second Dynasty
Heket Upright

1. The First Dynasty
Anubis Reversed

The subject of the reading is called Maggie. Maggie wishes to find out some more about the spiritual and material influences that are likely to be present or to emerge during her year ahead. She is hoping for an increase in the teaching work that she enjoys and also for greater prosperity in the next twelve months. She is also planning to spend time renovating her home. Her question is: *How can I best use my time and energy to bring me success, inner peace and personal fulfilment in the year to come?*

The stone tablets are placed into the bag and Maggie is asked to choose four of them, unseen, and place them in front of her in the arrangement described above. It is noted which stone tablets have been drawn in their upright position and which have been drawn in a reversed position. The reading is conducted towards the beginning of winter, so winter becomes the first period of enquiry for the purposes of this reading. The four stones drawn for Maggie's Secrets of the Sphinx spread are described overleaf.

1. THE FIRST DYNASTY (Winter)
Anubis Reversed

The winter is a time of training for Maggie, when she would be well advised to develop and hone her skills for the seasons to come. The training that comes with Anubis reversed is most likely to be one in healing, personal development, intuitive skills or psychic abilities; but it could also be in areas such as the management of people or the development of a new creative skill. This is a good time to read or do home courses.

The stone of Anubis in this position suggests that there is a need for Maggie to let go of the past and prepare herself for new challenges in the year ahead. It also indicates that she will be instrumental in furthering the healing or personal evolution of other people at this time. Vivid dreams, a strong sense of guidance and a feeling of being protected are all highlighted for this period. Maggie may focus on becoming the guide and protector for someone close to her as well as for herself.

2. THE SECOND DYNASTY (Spring)
Heket Upright

The spring is a time of new birth for Maggie. New opportunities are born from the healing and guidance of the previous season. This is an excellent time for Maggie to enjoy her home life and would be perfect for the renovation work she wishes to do. This renovation of bricks and mortar is fairly certain to go hand in hand with the renewal and strengthening of her family relationships. It is highly likely that career opportunities and increased prosperity will result from taking the time to establish a stronger home base both physically and emotionally. Maggie needs to concentrate upon what nourishes her and what can continue to nourish and sustain her for the months that follow.

The stone of Heket in this position blesses Maggie with a quickening of energy, intention and purpose. Something new is being born; this could include a new sense of security, a new feeling of harmony and an atmosphere of spiritual change. It is important that Maggie leaves herself some time for quiet contemplation because activity is likely to increase from this period onwards. This is also a time when new projects will come to life and increased prosperity and abundance could follow.

3. THE THIRD DYNASTY (Summer)
Khonsu Reversed

The summer is a time of youthful exuberance and celebration for Maggie. She will benefit from being light-hearted and spontaneous and she may find that she is drawn to people younger than herself or that she has the ability to awaken a feeling of youthfulness in people of all ages. If she is indeed teaching at this time then this is an excellent placing. It may indicate that she will find work with children and teenagers, or that she is particularly effective at making learning fun for people of all ages. However, the stone of Khonsu in this position also suggests that Maggie may choose to take some time away from work to experience a second childhood for herself, developing a playfulness that will uplift, enlighten and create fun for her friends and family.

The stone of Khonsu blesses Maggie with the ability to assist other people in dissolving their self-imposed restrictions, helping them to drop their seriousness and pretensions. Most people will appreciate and enjoy this, welcoming Maggie into their hearts; but not everyone is willing to let their hair down and play. Maggie would be wise to put a distance between herself and anyone who is committed to a more negative or restrictive view of the world. This is unlikely to be a great loss for her as there are many more people who will appreciate the influence that she has on their lives at this time.

4. THE FOURTH DYNASTY (Autumn)
Bastet Upright

The autumn is a time of balance and negotiation for Maggie. The fun and spontaneity of the summer gives way to a need for a milder, more even approach to life. Maggie is being encouraged to assert herself, gently but firmly, and be very clear about her needs and desires. It is an excellent time for negotiating with colleagues or employers, and rates of pay, working hours and conditions may be debated and agreed on now. It could also be a time for renegotiating personal and emotional commitments. Maggie would benefit from ensuring that she has enough time and space for herself, away from the needs or demands of others. By taking care of herself, she will have plenty of energy to be affectionate to the people who matter.

Bastet encourages Maggie to strengthen the personal rituals that help to balance and nourish her, keeping her free of stress. It is a favourable time to seek extra pampering or to implement a daily routine of meditation or quiet walks. This is a time of purification, when Maggie would be well advised to adjust any habits, beliefs or behaviour patterns that no longer suit her health and happiness. Relationships that do not support her ultimate goals or direction need to be renegotiated too, and anything outworn needs to be discarded. This is a time of sensuality and of purity. A heightened awareness of sensuality is likely to come with simple pleasures, and purity of purpose will bring a clearer picture of aims and aspirations in the year to follow. Evocative fragrances, the sense of smell and an awareness of personal space are all important now.

Overview

This is an excellent year for Maggie that begins with a period of preparation and develops into a time of new opportunities, fun and contentment. It is a constructive year, when career and home life can be built anew and foundations laid for future happiness. Work is available but needs to be balanced with play, quiet contemplation and time for personal development. The prosperity of the year comes with developing an overall quality of life rather than working constantly to increase finances while missing out on fun. The new projects, begun in the spring and developed through the summer, will continue to create prosperity in the years to come. The autumn is a time of self-healing that will prepare Maggie for the work that is to follow. Overall, a satisfying, joyful and peaceful year.

USING THE TREASURES OF THE PYRAMIDS SPREAD

The Treasures of the Pyramids is a five-stone spread laid out in the shape of a pyramid as seen from above. This represents the act of taking an overview of a particular situation or of seeing the bigger picture of life. The treasures that the pyramids have to offer are the secrets of the past, present and future in relation to the seeker's specific question or area of enquiry.

The Stone Tablets

The stones are drawn, unseen, from the bag. The first stone tablet represents the summit of the pyramid, and the four remaining stones represent the four corners, laid out clockwise from the bottom left.

THE TREASURES OF THE PYRAMIDS SPREAD

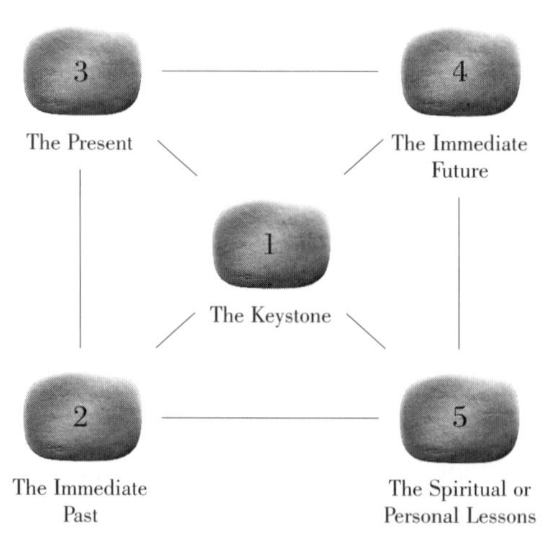

1. THE KEYSTONE

The first stone, at the centre of the spread, is the summit of the pyramid. It is the keystone and represents the seeker themselves. It is indicative of the seeker's role, aspirations and personality, shedding light upon the hopes, fears, wishes and underlying intentions that they bring to their current situation or focus of enquiry. As well as referring to the Upright or Reversed reading, as appropriate, it is important to refer to the Attributes section of the reading provided for the stone selected.

2. THE IMMEDIATE PAST

The second stone highlights the trends and influences of the immediate past in relation to the specific question or focus of enquiry. This does not necessarily represent a fixed period of time and often the timescale will need to be assessed for each reading in relation to the seeker's question. As a rough guide, I generally estimate it to be a period of approximately three months leading up to the time of the reading.

3. THE PRESENT

The third stone laid in the spread is indicative of the seeker's present position. This represents the physical, emotional or spiritual environment that the seeker currently inhabits and the challenges that they are facing in their life at this time.

4. THE IMMEDIATE FUTURE

The fourth stone of the Treasures of the Pyramids spread highlights the trends and influences the immediate future holds for the seeker in relation to the specific question or focus of enquiry. As with the stone of The Immediate Past, the period of time represented by this stone tablet is not necessarily fixed, but in general terms can be seen as a period of three months from the present moment onwards.

5. THE SPIRITUAL OR PERSONAL LESSONS

The fifth and last stone of this spread is indicative of the spiritual or personal lessons that the seeker is receiving from his or her current situation and area of enquiry. It highlights the best that can be achieved in the situation and the personal growth that is available. This stone points the seeker towards the most promising course of action for them to take.

SAMPLE READING

The subject of the reading is called Sam. Sam is in a long-term relationship that, although loving, does not currently fulfil some of his sexual and emotional needs. He is both happy with the life that he and his girlfriend have developed together and frustrated because he does not know how to handle the needs that are not being addressed within this relationship. He does not wish to be unfaithful to his partner but, equally, he does not know how to continue living with the sexual and emotional discrepancy that exists. His question is: *Should I stay in this relationship and search for new solutions or separate and start out again on my own?*

The stone tablets are placed into the bag and Sam is asked to choose five of them, unseen, and place them in front of him as shown on the previous page. It is noted which stone tablets have been drawn in their upright position and which have been drawn in a reversed position.

1. THE KEYSTONE

Apis Upright

This stone indicates that Sam is experiencing an expansion of his personal power and has many opportunities to express his spiritual purpose and special gifts in ways that can have a practical impact on the world. Within the relationship in question, he is amiable and easy going; able to accept the situation very well and provide support and stability for his partner. Sam's strength and emotional resilience allow him to cope extremely well, but may also enable him to ignore his own needs for sustained periods of time. This may not be so healthy.

The stone of Apis is representative of messages. Sam may be responding to internal messages telling him that it is time to move on to new challenges and new ways of viewing the world. This may be contributing to his feelings of restlessness within the relationship. Sam is eager to develop his special gifts and talents, and he has a strong desire to fulfil his spiritual purpose. It is possible that he cannot fulfil his underlying purpose within his domestic situation as it currently stands. Some change in his relationship is indicated, although this could be a change of communication and attitude rather than a complete separation.

2. THE IMMEDIATE PAST

Re Upright

The stone of Re indicates that Sam has recently passed through a very creative, uplifting and joyful period of his life. He has been blessed with an abundance of creative energy and an increase in physical stamina and drive. Sam may have received a great deal of positive attention from friends, family and colleagues as his charismatic influence increased.

While these positive influences would have helped to sustain Sam through his relationship difficulties they may also have highlighted the discrepancies that existed within his domestic situation. As his energy increased, his sexual or emotional frustrations may also have increased. As his influence and creative power expanded, they may have highlighted the areas of his life that could appear to be in decline or stuck. New doors opening in some areas of Sam's life, in his career for instance, could easily have given him the desire to open new doors within his intimate relationships and emotional expression.

3. THE PRESENT
Seth Upright

Seth in this position indicates that the present is indeed a time for Sam to create a new order in his life. It may appear to be a very chaotic period when every aspect of Sam's life and relationships comes into question. Old ways of relating to his girlfriend do not work for Sam now and the tried and tested methods of resolving or living with the discrepancies in sexual and emotional need do not bring an easy resolution. As disturbing and as disruptive as this period may feel to Sam and to his partner, it is filled with growth and opportunity for them both.

The stone of Seth can indicate that Sam's higher awareness is radically asserting itself and his greater purpose is emerging to send ripples of dramatic change through every aspect of his life. Many positive changes can come from the conflict that exists within the relationship, within the present situation and, most importantly, within Sam himself. The divinatory meaning of this stone stimulates a discussion that helps Sam to examine his motives, desires and choices at this time. He is given a space to talk about and weigh up his conflicting thoughts and feelings.

Sam realizes that his desire to make his relationship work is very strong. If he was absolutely convinced that this relationship was wrong for him or that his life would be better elsewhere, he would probably have made the break before now. He is still very committed to his partner and he still benefits from the relationship in many ways, despite his frustrations. Seth reminds us that extraordinary compromises can be reached and that it is the conflict and not the solution that facilitates the most spectacular personal and spiritual growth.

In general terms, the stone of Seth in this position could indicate a separation or, equally, it could indicate a major shake up in a relationship that allows for a new and better understanding to emerge. Either is possible, but Sam's personality and overall tendencies would suggest that he is likely to take the latter course, at least for the time being. Clarification of this can come from the two stones that follow.

4. THE IMMEDIATE FUTURE
Amun Reversed

This stone indicates that Sam is moving into a period of his life when he will quite clearly put the needs of others ahead of his own. His fulfilment and satisfaction will come through giving to others and supporting them with their growth and development, even if this means putting aside his own desires and ambitions for the time being. The suggestion is that he will be very successful once he has taken his attention away from his own success and placed it squarely on the service that he can give to others.

The stone of Amun suggests that Sam's focus is about to shift from his needs that are not being addressed within the relationship, to the pleasure that he can derive from putting the needs of his girlfriend first. The sexual and emotional discrepancies that have been a focus of conflict will become less important. Instead, the greater good of the relationship and, perhaps, the friendships and family connections associated with both parties will become the focus of consideration. Sam's girlfriend may need his support during this period and he will gain great satisfaction and spiritual advancement from providing it. This is not to suggest that Sam's needs are to be ignored, repressed or put to one side indefinitely. They will just hold less importance for Sam for a while and they may even be better addressed because of Sam's change of attitude.

Sam would benefit from thinking of himself as a guardian angel and continuing to seek creative solutions to the situation he is living within. How can his presence be of benefit to others, his girlfriend included? How can he continue to give of himself from a position of strength and good grace, whilst acknowledging his own feelings, rather than from a state of martyrdom, self-denial and bitterness? This stone suggests that, in giving of himself, Sam is able to find extraordinary solutions that help him to transcend his current dilemma. His service will not only benefit others, it will bring him an abundance of unexpected and magical rewards.

5. THE SPIRITUAL OR PERSONAL LESSONS

Geb Reversed

This final stone tablet brings us to the crux of the matter and highlights the spiritual or personal lessons that Sam is currently facing. Choosing Geb reversed in this position would indicate that Sam is learning about leadership, authority and responsibility. His current situation could be strengthening the leadership qualities within him. By living through the challenges that he is facing in his relationship, Sam will be better able to provide leadership and guidance for others facing similar challenges. This situation is constantly stimulating Sam to examine his personal responsibility for his own needs and the joint responsibility that he and his girlfriend have for the success and well-being of them both.

Geb is the god of the earth and, as such, he can provide us with the earthly lessons of survival, sustenance and nourishment. Our efforts to sustain and nourish ourselves and to provide for the people we love can facilitate much of our spiritual learning and growth. In Sam's case, this may indicate that the nourishment and stability that he provides for his girlfriend is helping them both to grow. It also suggests that he would benefit from placing less attention upon the needs that are not being met within his relationship and more attention upon the abundance of material and emotional sustenance that his girlfriend is able to provide for him.

This is a stone of great fertility which indicates that there are rich opportunities for new growth and new solutions. It is also a stone of paternal authority which suggests that there are roots to this dilemma and clues to potential solutions contained within Sam's relationship with a father or grandfather figure. Perhaps Sam is repeating a pattern of frustration within relationships that is similar to his own father or grandfather.

Alternatively, he could be rebelling against the choices, advice or expectations of a prominent male role model.

If, for example, Sam's father stayed in an unhappy marriage from a sense of duty, it is possible that Sam may fear becoming trapped in a similar situation. This fear may equally contribute to Sam creating his own frustrating relationships or breaking from a relationship at the earliest signs of difficulty, rather than being committed to finding a satisfying solution. Sam may need to be reassured that while he is blessed with the positive qualities he has inherited or learned from his father figure, he does not have to either repeat or rebel against the patterns he observed when growing up. He has the ability to create new opportunities and solutions that are unique to him.

Overview

The stone tablets chosen for this reading could either indicate a separation or a radical change within a relationship that will endure and thrive. Either outcome is possible, but Sam's personality and the nature of the realizations he makes about himself during this reading would suggest that he is committed to staying with his girlfriend and finding ways to make the relationship work. Either way, the relationship is in a process of dramatic change and Sam would be well advised to communicate as fully as possible with his partner. He could seek solutions by:

- Acknowledging himself and his girlfriend for what they have created together; focusing on the positive, fulfilling aspects of this.
- Focusing his attention on what he can actively provide for his girlfriend rather than just on his own needs.
- Doing his best to communicate his needs to his girlfriend without blame or recrimination. Good communication does not come about from apportioning blame to one or both parties but, instead, comes from an honest exchange of needs and feelings. Sam would benefit from a willingness to listen, build on what is working in the relationship and negotiate some mutually satisfying improvements.
- Seeking relationship counselling, for himself and his girlfriend, with experienced counsellors who are able to provide constructive mediation and, perhaps, some sessions with a sex therapist.
- Seeking individual counselling. This may be useful if Sam's girlfriend will not agree to relationship counselling or if he needs additional space to clarify his thoughts and feelings before implementing changes in his domestic situation.
- Finding new ways to nourish and fulfil his own needs which do not place demands on his girlfriend.
- Reviewing his situation in about six months' time. Sam may then be in a better position to decide whether the relationship is continuing to grow or whether it is continuing to frustrate or disappoint him. If he has made a genuine effort to find new solutions and he does not feel that he has been able to facilitate mutually satisfying changes, he may then decide to go ahead with a process of separation. However, the reading would suggest that this is unlikely to be the case.

USING THE RELATIONSHIP SPREAD

The Relationship spread is a spread of two stones that brings illumination and clarity to any given relationship. It does this by highlighting the underlying forces or spiritual dynamics that are operating within the alliance. It provides the seeker with useful insights into his or her family relationships, friendships, business partnerships and romantic involvements. A new awareness can be brought to relationships from the past, present and future.

The Stone Tablets

Two stone tablets are drawn, unseen, from the bag. They are then laid before the seeker from left to right.

THE RELATIONSHIP SPREAD

Yourself in the Relationship

The Other in the Relationship

1. YOURSELF IN THE RELATIONSHIP

The first stone to be drawn is stone of Yourself in the Relationship. It represents the person who is seeking guidance, indicating their hopes, aspirations, tendencies and predominant personality traits in connection with the relationship in question. It also represents their underlying role within the relationship and the spiritual influence they are likely to have on the other person featured in this particular spread.

It is important to note that this stone tablet is only representative of the seeker within this one, specific relationship and, as such, is not to be thought of as a general representation of the individual. However, if this stone turns up again and again to represent the seeker in other readings or if it is one of the seven stones selected in their Eye of Horus spread, then it is likely to provide a wider representation of their personality and spiritual potential.

If this stone is placed upright then refer to the text for the Upright reading and Attributes of the stone tablet selected. If this stone is reversed then refer to the text for the Reversed reading and Attributes of the stone tablet selected.

2. THE OTHER IN THE RELATIONSHIP

This stone represents the second person within the relationship. It reflects this person in the same way that the first stone reflects the seeker. It indicates their underlying role within the relationship in question and the spiritual influence that they are likely to have on the seeker.

It is important to note that this stone tablet is only representative of this person within this one, specific, relationship and, as such, is not to be thought of as a general representation of them.

If this stone is upright then refer to the Upright and Attributes readings of the stone selected. If it is reversed then refer to the Reversed and Attributes readings.

SAMPLE READING ONE

1. Yourself in the Relationship
Horus Upright

2. The Other in the Relationship
Isis Upright

The subject of the reading is called Diane. She is wishing to develop a greater understanding of the underlying spiritual connection between herself and her young son. Diane is thirty-two years of age; her son, Simeon, is six. She has a belief in reincarnation and suspects that she and Simeon are continuing a relationship that they began in a previous existence. Her question is: *What is the underlying spiritual connection between my son and myself and why have we chosen to be together in this lifetime?*

The stone tablets are placed into the bag and Diane is asked to choose two of them, unseen, and place them in front of her, noting if they are upright or reversed. The first stone chosen represents Diane herself and the second stone represents her son.

1. YOURSELF IN THE RELATIONSHIP
Horus Upright

This stone tablet shows Diane to be a positive, visionary influence for her young son. She helps him to see the bigger picture of life and to enjoy the fun and freedom of the world around him. Rather than being overprotective of her son, Diane is able to stimulate him to be adventurous and to help him to widen his horizons. The stone of Horus indicates that motherhood is positive and evolutionary for Diane too. Her relationship with Simeon allows her to become the sovereign of her own life and it provides her with a level of support and protection that boosts her confidence. Her ability to communicate is strengthened and, rather than feeling restricted and burdened by having a young child to take care of, the responsibility is liberating for her and helps her to fulfil her spiritual destiny. In short, having Simeon as her son helps Diane to feel more youthful, alive and purposeful.

2. THE OTHER IN THE RELATIONSHIP
Isis Upright

This stone tablet shows Simeon to be highly protective of his mother. He is very devoted to her and his loyalty helps to bring out her best qualities, allowing her to be more extrovert and confident. Simeon is likely to be naturally wise and ingenious in responding to Diane's needs and feelings. His presence gives her life greater meaning and purpose. He has a magical and engaging personality that makes him an excellent companion.

The stone of Isis indicates that Simeon may have a tendency to be a parent for older and younger members of his family alike, and especially for his own mother. He is a very astute, powerful character who is both strong willed and extremely compassionate. While his natural maturity needs to be acknowledged and respected, so does his right to be a child. Diane would serve him well by allowing him to assume a degree of responsibility for his own choices from an early age, but she would be doing him a disservice if she leant upon him too much, or expected him to provide the kind of emotional support that she would be best to seek from other adults.

Overview

The stone tablets of Horus and Isis together indicate a very powerful union indeed. It is interesting to note that there is a suggestion of a role reversal in this mother–son relationship. The mother, Diane, is represented by the royal son, Horus, while her offspring is represented by the powerful maternal archetype, Isis. This is not uncommon in parent–child relationships, with many children being born with greater innate wisdom, insight and strength than their forebears. Numerous children 'parent' their own mother or father.

From a reincarnational perspective, this combination of stones would suggest that these two souls have been together before. A previous relationship would probably have had a similar spiritual dynamic, although, physically, Simeon is more likely to have been the parent and Diane the child.

Simeon's presence in Diane's life does allow her to fulfil her personal destiny and provides her with a sense of purpose that stimulates her visionary gifts. She may even discover that she has clairvoyant or psychic abilities. Diane's presence in Simeon's life stimulates him to strengthen his innate awareness and expands his view of the world. His relationship with her may even provide him with a sense that he is able to complete unfinished business and set the world to rights. The union will be happy and fulfilling for him too.

The spiritual role reversal implied here illustrates how our obvious, external appearance can differ from our underlying, spiritual identity, purpose and potential.

SAMPLE READING TWO

1. Yourself in the Relationship
Anat Reversed

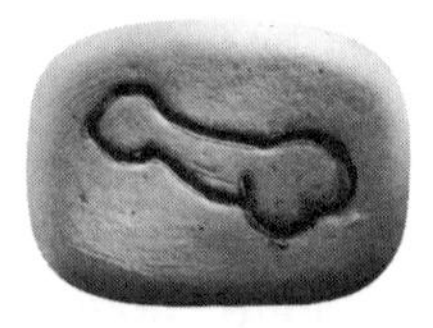

2. The Other in the Relationship
Min Upright

The subject of this reading is called Rachel. Rachel has met a man at work to whom she is attracted. His name is John and he was recently transferred to Rachel's department from another branch of the same company. Although they have only been working together for a short period of time, and they do not know each other very well, they do seem to have a great deal in common. What is more, they are both single and John has indicated that he is interested in spending time with Rachel outside of office hours. Her question is: *Would it be best to keep this relationship on a professional basis and continue to view John as a colleague, or is it appropriate for me to allow a deeper friendship to develop between us?*

The stone tablets are placed into the bag and Rachel is asked to choose two of them, unseen, and place them in front of her. The first stone represents Rachel and the second stone represents her colleague, John. It is carefully noted whether the stones are positioned upright or reversed, and the appropriate readings are referred to.

1. YOURSELF IN THE RELATIONSHIP

Anat Reversed

This stone shows Rachel to be an extremely passionate, fearless and impulsive force within this relationship. Her motivation is powerfully sexual and her influence on John may be highly motivational, enthusiastic and even aggressive. She has the potential to stir John into taking direct, passionate action. This could be a very positive state of affairs if the relationship is kept on a professional level. Carefully directed passion could prove to be a distinct advantage for their partnership, giving them both the energy and zeal to further their careers.

If Rachel pushes John into developing a more intimate relationship with her, the stone of Anat indicates that she is likely to succeed in creating an explosively passionate union. However, as her motivation is predominantly sexual, she does need to exercise a little caution. Does she have the emotional stability to handle herself at work when her relationship with John becomes more intimate? Do they really have enough in common to create a balanced, stable relationship that will be sustainable and that will not disrupt their careers? This stone shows that Rachel could easily push John into a liaison that he is not ready for. There is likely to be fun and excitement but there could be fireworks too.

2. THE OTHER IN THE RELATIONSHIP

Min Upright

This stone tablet shows John to be as sexually motivated as Rachel. He is ready to drop his inhibitions and engage in a carefree sexual relationship. He does not really need to be pushed into having an affair as he already has a heightened sense of pleasure and celebration. Rachel's influence just stimulates the passion that John is ready to express and explore at this time. Love, laughter and physical sensuality are all relevant for John, and Rachel is an appropriate person for him to share this with. It is also likely that his involvement with Rachel will be guilt free for him and will not affect his career adversely.

The stone of Min indicates that John is at a stage when he feels that he is ready for an affair with Rachel. However, this does not indicate that the relationship has the potential to mature into something more substantial. Either way, it would appear that John's life will be positively stimulated by Rachel rather than being disrupted. He will be a fun and passionate lover for her and, in return, she will have an exciting, transformational influence upon him.

Overview

The stone tablets of Anat and Min together indicate that a passionate union with John is almost inevitable. However, Rachel does need to think carefully about her situation and the consequences for her emotional life and professional status. At this stage, she could still choose to keep her relationship with John as a passionate professional union that could inspire them both to achieve great things within their careers. This is still possible if they engage in a sexual relationship, but there are many more risks and complications involved, and this combination of stones shows that Rachel is more likely to encounter a degree of frustration in mixing work and pleasure than John is.

If John and Rachel did not work together, these stones would indicate a wonderfully positive sexual union that has every chance of developing into something interesting, if not, necessarily, long term. If Rachel is looking for something more substantial then she would benefit from taking her time, keeping him interested, but not plunging in until they have established a stronger friendship. Because of the professional connection between them, caution and discretion is to be advised. However, judging by these two stone tablets, it is unlikely that sensible advice will be followed in this instance. Life is, after all, more fun when we take a few risks!

SOME OTHER USES OF THIS SPREAD

There are many ways in which the Relationship spread can be used to bring insight and understanding to a relationship between any two given people. It can be referred to by a couple together to examine the current influences present within their relationship. Each person can pick the individual stone that represents him or her in the partnership. The two stones are then compared together in a similar fashion to the examples detailed above. This method would be equally appropriate for friendships, business relationships, family connections and romantic involvements.

This spread can also be used by an individual to examine the influences present within a relationship that has powerfully affected the course of her or his life. If you wish to practise this then the obvious example is to choose stones at random to represent your parents or parent figures. The first stone could be your mother, the second your father and a third stone could be added to represent you in relation to your parents.

Powerful Combinations of Stone Tablets

Some of the gods and goddesses represented by the stone tablets have unique and powerful relationships. The impact of these stones when drawn together in a Relationship spread is greater than the individual divinatory meanings of the stones when drawn alone. Here are just a selection of stone tablets that, when chosen together, can indicate a particularly powerful relationship. There are many more powerful combinations that you will discover as you use *The Eye of Horus*.

GEB AND NUT

This is a grandfather–grandmother (Nut–Geb) relationship. It indicates a couple of wise, mature individuals who complement and balance each other perfectly. One provides more of the stability in the relationship while the other provides more of the impetus for growth and expansion. This is an excellent combination for a marriage partnership because it indicates that the couple in question will continue to develop together over a sustained period of time, although this means that it is good for most other long-term partnerships too. This combination can also indicate a well established partnership that has been carried over from a previous life.

APIS AND IMHOTEP

This is a strong father–son (Apis–Imhotep) relationship. Within this combination Apis is representative of the creator god Ptah who was the father of Imhotep in the Memphis triad. This can be the basis for an excellent business partnership, indicating the effective teamwork that can come from having a similarity of goals and objectives. Both parties can 'immortalize' themselves through their work, achieving both spiritual and material success. They both have strong communication skills although the person represented by Apis is more likely to be the salesperson, chairperson, figurehead or public relations officer, while the person represented by Imhotep is more likely to be the creative inspiration as the draughtsman or woman, project manager, technician or artistic or literary genius. The Apis figure would probably be the senior partner and the Imhotep figure the junior partner who provides the know-how, although, in reality, their roles are equal and complementary.

If a couple who are married or in a long-term relationship were to select this combination of stones, then it would indicate that they work together very effectively as a team, and could consider running a business together if they do not already do so.

AMUN AND RE

This is an excellent combination that indicates a relationship of strength, power and extraordinary creativity. This is a good political or a creative partnership of charismatic individuals who are both very effective in their own right, but when working together their abilities are multiplied, allowing their influence to extend further than if they chose to go it alone. This is a passionate pairing where each person is fired up by the enthusiasm of the other. There may be some clashes of ego as both people in this relationship love to be the driving force and the recipient of recognition. However, these areas of competition can generally be resolved. The person represented by Amun may become the more powerful of the two, but the person represented by Re is more likely to be the centre of attention. They need to learn to share both the power and the limelight for this relationship to reach its full potential.

SOME OTHER POWERFUL COMBINATIONS

	Key Concepts
OSIRIS AND ISIS	Good marriage, Loving union, Fulfilment of spiritual potential
SETH AND NEPHTHYS	Conflicting interests, Estrangement, Fulfilment of individual destiny
OSIRIS AND HORUS	Father–son relationship, Spiritual closeness contrasted by physical or emotional distance, Similarity of purpose, Succession
OSIRIS AND NEPHTHYS	Brotherly or sisterly relationship, Pleasurable liaison, Seduction, Family loyalty
ISIS AND NEPHTHYS	Sisterhood or brotherhood, Trust, Family support, Complementary interests, Empathy
KHNUM AND HAPY	Prosperity, Abundance, Favourable partnership, New projects, Creative union, Spiritual enhancement, Professional support

USING THE EYE OF HORUS SPREAD

The Eye of Horus spread is a cast of seven stone tablets, laid out in the shape of an eye. This spread is a personal totem of power, creativity and spiritual purpose that is normally cast for an individual only once, but can be referred back to many times as the basis for other readings and as an essential personal reference. It provides a useful focus for questions that arise or when a deeper insight is required. This is a spread of illumination that highlights what is already known about the seeker's life path, while revealing what is unseen; bringing knowledge and awareness of hidden talents, special gifts and spiritual purpose. It reveals aspects of the spiritual blueprint that we have chosen from, or even before, birth and that we are playing out through our lifetime.

It is useful to first develop a degree of familiarity with the stones and the spiritual archetypes that they each represent before embarking upon a reading that utilizes the Eye of Horus spread. It often helps to practise with the other spreads described in this section first so that you can learn to combine the text with your intuition and begin to create your own style as a reader of the stone tablets. It also helps to create and read this spread for yourself before agreeing to do it for other people. In this way you can familiarize yourself with some of the complexities, nuances and depths of the spiritual archetypes that can be present in a reading of this kind.

How to Begin

With the Eye of Horus spread it is especially important to create the right atmosphere. So, remember to choose your environment and create your 'sacred space' with care. To do this reading properly you will need plenty of time. I would suggest at least forty-five minutes if you are doing the reading for yourself and at least an hour if you are doing it for somebody else.

READING FOR YOURSELF

If you are doing this reading for yourself then you will need a pen and paper or a tape recorder to make a record of the positions of the stone tablets and any flashes of inspiration that you receive. Because this is normally a 'one off' reading, the more time you give yourself to digest it, the more sense it will make to you later when you utilize it as an important personal reference. Keeping a clear record will be of great benefit.

READING FOR SOMEONE ELSE

When reading for another person it is best to have both a pen and paper and a tape recorder. With the pen and paper you can record the positions of the stones for future use and with the tape recorder you can record your reading and the dialogue between you and the person seeking guidance. As with the previous spreads, disregard this if the seeker does not wish to have or is not comfortable with a recording.

The Stone Tablets

The stones are drawn, unseen, and spread in the shape of an eye as shown below. The first stone represents the pupil and the remaining six stones circle it from the top-right corner in a clockwise direction. Each stone tablet highlights an aspect of the seeker's essential, spiritual blueprint. This blueprint encompasses the spiritual origins of the seeker, the lessons to be learnt within this lifetime and the ultimate spiritual direction that would follow from the choices that the seeker has made up to the present moment.

The centre and right side of the spread, stones one, two, three and four, highlight what is already seen, the spiritual origins, basic personality traits and underlying choices of the seeker. The left side of the spread, stones five, six and seven, highlight what is unseen, the life lessons ahead and the ultimate spiritual direction of the seeker.

THE EYE OF HORUS SPREAD

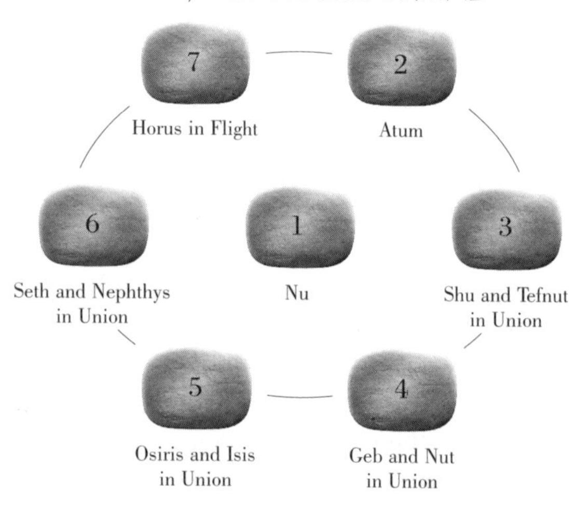

1. NU

The first stone is placed at the centre of the eye, where the pupil would be. The stone of Nu tells a story of the essential nature of the soul, how it existed at the dawn of creation or at the beginning of this lifetime and the innate qualities that propelled it from formlessness and into life. This is the seeker in his or her purest form. This is also the basic personality with its drives, motivations and unique creative potential. As well as representing our spiritual origins the stone of Nu represents one aspect of our ultimate spiritual direction. We come from formlessness into life and we return to formlessness, regaining our true identity, when the lessons of this lifetime are complete.

If this stone is placed upright then refer to the text for the Upright reading and Attributes of the stone tablet selected. If this stone is reversed then refer to the text for the Reversed reading and Attributes.

The stone of Nu that we draw in our Eye of Horus spread holds particular significance for us whenever we draw it, either on an individual basis or as part of another spread. It is a valuable tool for ongoing contemplation and clarification through our lives. Regular practice of the meditation and positive affirmations that are included for use with this stone will assist us in awakening the power of our true nature.

2. ATUM

The second stone is placed above the first and slightly to the right. The stone of Atum tells of the outer personality, the faces, external qualities and strengths that the seeker has assumed in the world. This is the stone that tells us how we have created ourselves, the impact that our presence has upon other people and how we are viewed.

The stone of Atum is also the stone of childhood and it may remind us of our early lessons, dramas, relationships and successes. Many of these traits and influences may still be operating within our adult lives.

If this stone tablet is placed upright then refer to the text for the Upright reading. If it is reversed then refer to the text for the Reversed reading.

3. SHU AND TEFNUT IN UNION

The third stone represents the right corner of the eye. This is the stone of Shu and Tefnut in Union, it tells us about the atmosphere and the environment that we create around ourselves. Where have we chosen to learn our most powerful life lessons? Who are the people we attract to us? What are the predominant feelings and emotions we carry with us? What are the basic beliefs and attitudes that we colour our lives with and that influence the choices we make? Shu is the god of air and Tefnut is the goddess of moisture. This stone represents the air and moisture of our lives; the bubble of consciousness that we carry with us to support the lessons that we have chosen for ourselves.

This stone tablet also relates to the period of the seeker's life from puberty to adulthood. It is, therefore, indicative of our place within the family unit and of how we develop our independence from our family so that we may establish our own personality and make our mark upon the world.

If this stone is placed upright then refer to the text for the Upright reading. If it is reversed then refer to the text for the Reversed reading.

4. GEB AND NUT IN UNION

The fourth stone is the stone of Geb and Nut in Union. It is indicative of our spiritual range: our 'earth and sky'.

This is the basic range of spiritual lessons that we have chosen for ourselves in this lifetime. It provides a general blueprint for our spiritual and material development.

The 'earth' aspect is the spiritual learning that comes to us through our basic survival, our relationship to the material world and to our body and emotions. The 'sky' aspect is the spiritual learning that comes through our spiritual vision, our relationship to the non-physical realms and our relationship to our mind and higher reason.

For this stone only, refer to the text for both the Upright and the Reversed reading. If this stone is placed upright then refer to the text for the Upright reading as the 'sky' and the text for the Reversed reading as the 'earth'. As a general rule, an upright stone in this position will indicate that the greatest learning can be achieved through our relationship to other people, action and activity, although this does not exclude our relationship to ourselves, stillness and contemplation as important to our development. If this stone is reversed then refer to the text for the Reversed reading as the 'sky' and the text for the Upright reading as the 'earth'. As a general rule, a reversed stone in this position will indicate that the greatest learning can be achieved through our relationship to ourselves, through stillness and contemplation, although this does not exclude relationships to others, action and activity as important to our development.

5. OSIRIS AND ISIS IN UNION

The fifth stone is the stone of Osiris and Isis in Union. It indicates our personal power, our special gifts, our sovereignty and our birthright. This is the role or position that we have come into life to create or inherit. This stone tablet represents our path to immortality: the meeting of our unique magic (Isis) with our universal power (Osiris). This union brings about the fulfilment of our divine purpose.

This stone also relates to the predominant roles that we undertake in our adult lives and the contributions that we make to the world around us.

If this stone is placed upright then refer to the text for the Upright reading. If it is reversed then refer to the text for the Reversed reading.

6. SETH AND NEPHTHYS IN UNION

The sixth stone is positioned on the far left of the spread, representing the left corner of the eye. The stone of Seth and Nephthys in Union indicates our greatest challenges, both externally and internally. It may represent an aspect of our lives or our personalities that appears to be out of control or that is beyond our ability to control. It demonstrates our greatest paths to self-healing and represents the forces that we attract to ourselves to stimulate the wholeness that we seek. This could be seen as our shadow side of unacknowledged or conflicting feelings that are growing towards the light of acceptance and integration.

This stone also relates to the hidden roles that we undertake in our adult lives, the personality traits that we keep from ourselves or our private persona. This could include our secret fantasies or hidden fears. These aspects of our personalities need to be recognized and addressed if we are to fulfil our spiritual potential.

If this stone tablet is placed upright then refer to the text for the Upright reading. If it is reversed then refer to the text for the Reversed reading.

7. HORUS IN FLIGHT

This final stone tablet in the Eye of Horus spread is the stone of Horus in Flight. This is the stone of our ultimate spiritual direction, based on the influences and choices that have preceded it. Linked with the stone of Nu, our origins and essential self, it provides a picture of what we are growing towards in this lifetime. It is the expansion and integration of the qualities linked to these two stones that provide us with the greatest picture of our ultimate goal. However, the divinatory meanings that are provided within this book can only give us a glimpse of this goal. The full picture goes beyond words; it is there to be learnt and discovered.

This stone tablet is representative of our vision and our higher consciousness. It is symbolic of our flight towards our highest potential. It is indicative of the great maturity and eternal youthfulness that can be achieved when we follow our bliss and do our best to live a life of creativity, integrity, love and joy.

If this stone is placed upright then refer to the text for the Upright reading and Attributes of the stone tablet selected. If this stone is reversed then refer to the text for the Reversed reading and Attributes of the stone tablet selected.

Just like the stone of Nu, our stone of Horus in Flight holds particular significance for us whenever we draw it, whether it is on an individual basis or as part of another spread. This stone is a valuable tool for our ongoing contemplation and clarification. Regular practice of the Meditation and Positive Affirmations that are included for use with this stone will assist us in awakening the power of our true nature and our ultimate direction.

The Ongoing Use of This Spread

Please note that the concepts and issues linked to the Eye of Horus spread are the most universal of all the spreads detailed within this book. When conducting a reading it may be necessary to adapt some of the language or ideas in the Upright or Reversed readings that are more concerned with day-to-day occurrences to suit the greater picture of the seeker's life and spiritual development. The spirit of the stone tablets is more important than specific words or phrases. This spread, more than any other, is concerned with stimulating new questions rather than providing the seeker with rigid answers to a specific enquiry. When referred to again and again, it may arouse a greater understanding of the sacred archetypes that have been chosen and the meaning that they hold for the individual seeker.

From time to time it is useful to lay out the stone tablets that you have chosen in their 'eye' position and read through the text for each one again. Each time you examine this personal blueprint you are likely to understand more about your innate power, your underlying choices and your greater potential in this lifetime.

Choosing any of these seven stone tablets within another reading when you are casting one of the other spreads or when you are using stones individually is particularly significant. This is especially so when you place the stone in the same orientation, upright or reversed, as it appears in your Eye of Horus spread.

Whenever these stones turn up they are reminding you of your underlying spiritual choices and urging you to be true to your higher purpose.

The stone tablet that you most identify with from the Eye of Horus spread can be used as a valuable starting point for other spreads. You could instinctively choose any of these seven stones to represent your present position, rather than choosing one at random, when you are using the Wisdom of Maat spread or The Secrets of the Sphinx spread and to represent you in a Relationship spread. Just place the appropriate stone into position and randomly choose the other stones as normal to complete the spread.

SAMPLE READING

7. Horus in Flight
Nephthys Upright

2. Atum
Meretseger Reversed

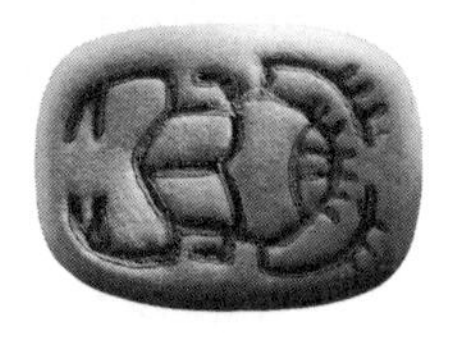

6. Seth and Nephthys in Union
Khepri Reversed

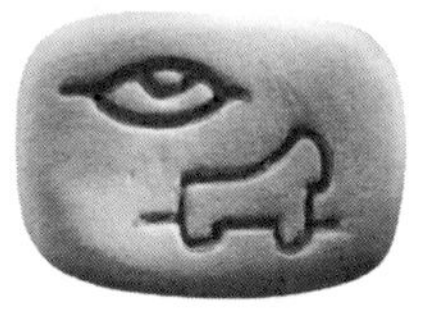

1. Nu
Osiris Upright

3. Shu and Tefnut in Union
Horus Upright

5. Osiris and Isis in Union
Isis Upright

4. Geb and Nut in Union
Seth Upright

The subject of the reading is called Judith. Judith is seeking clarification of her overall direction and she wants to be reminded of her spiritual choices and gifts. She is also wishing to explore the reasons for some of the events of the past and to make sense of her future options. Judith is forty-one, bright, vivacious and friendly, although she is carrying some old sadness that does not seem to relate to her current view of the world and the relationships that she has created. Her statement of intention is: *I would like to know more about my spiritual purpose and my path to happiness and fulfilment.*

Judith chooses seven of the stones from the bag, unseen, and places them in front of her. The reader notes the order and lays the stones in the eye configuration.

1. NU
Osiris Upright

This stone tablet shows Judith to have a strong awareness of continuing life and may indicate that the spiritual lessons she has chosen for herself in this lifetime are a direct continuation of lessons that have been brought forward from a previous life. In short, she may be resolving unfinished business.

The stone of Osiris in this position indicates that Judith is an essentially positive person who naturally views the world with trust and positive anticipation. Life is viewed as a fertile place of learning and the world is rich with an abundance of opportunities. Judith is blessed with evergreen youthfulness and a sense of universal power. She has an innate belief in the ongoing process of life and an awareness that even setbacks or events that may appear to be disastrous will ultimately fuel her spiritual and material success. At a soul level, Judith has developed enough of her innate strengths to know that she is capable of handling most things and that she can embrace the adventure of life with a degree of confidence in her own abilities.

2. ATUM

Meretseger Reversed

This stone tablet shows Judith to be a compassionate, merciful person who is generally forgiving of other people. She has a natural gift for freeing herself from mistakes, conflicts and judgemental relationships because she herself is willing to forgive and move on. Her approach to life brings her clarity and peace of mind and she presents a face to the world that is generally open and accepting of other people. The stone of Meretseger in this position also indicates that Judith's childhood was filled with compassion and forgiveness. These may be qualities that she learned from her parents or they may be qualities that she herself developed to overcome childhood challenges or problems. Meretseger in this position, either upright or reversed, may indicate a childhood of seclusion and, indeed, Judith's upbringing was quite protected and isolated.

3. SHU AND TEFNUT IN UNION

Horus Upright

This stone indicates that Judith creates an atmosphere of balance and communication wherever she goes. She has a tendency to choose emotional and physical environments that allow for an extensive exchange of ideas and information which she thrives on. However, she instinctively knows when to retreat to somewhere calm and secluded so that she can keep herself in balance and listen to her inner messages. She may have an affinity with wild, untamed places and a belief that she has a powerful role to play in this lifetime.

The stone of Horus in this position also indicates that Judith's adolescence was a period of great expansion when her visionary abilities and communication skills grew in strength and brilliance. The influence of Horus would also suggest that, although Judith has had to work at proving herself in the world and establishing herself as a person in her own right, she was well supported in doing so. She was nurtured and protected as she expanded her awareness and established her sovereign right to be in charge of her own destiny.

4. GEB AND NUT IN UNION

Seth Upright

The Sky (the upright reading) This stone tablet indicates that Judith has the potential to create a radical new order in her mind and higher consciousness. This is a lifetime that will be filled with dramatic changes, within and without. Judith may experience periods of mental or spiritual turmoil from which she will emerge stronger, wiser, healthier and more aligned to her higher self. Old patterns of thought and outmoded beliefs will be discarded as new ideas revolutionize Judith's relationship to herself.

Judith's skills of balanced communication, compassion, forgiveness and optimism, that have already been discussed, would prevent this placing from becoming too disruptive or too chaotic.

The Earth (the reversed reading) The stone of Seth in this position also indicates that Judith's greatest potential for spiritual learning comes from acting as a force for dramatic change in the world. She may choose jobs or roles that allow her to disrupt the old order and replace it with the space for something new and more effective to grow. Judith would be well advised to avoid getting bogged down in petty power struggles. She may also experience some dramatic physical or material changes in her life.

One of Judith's greatest lessons in this lifetime is to balance the desire for dramatic change with a recognition that there is a need to create solutions that allow everyone to win. The previous stone tablets in this reading would indicate that she has many qualities that would help her to achieve this.

This placing is perfect for a social activist, a politician or anyone else involved with revolutionary changes, be they in the arts or the sciences.

5. OSIRIS AND ISIS IN UNION

Isis Upright

This stone tablet has a particularly powerful placing because it strengthens the influence of Isis in this spread and therefore in Judith's life. Although she can operate extremely well in partnership with the lover or consort of her choice, this placing would indicate that Judith's special gifts are particularly enhanced when she assumes a maternal role, or when she acts autonomously or independently of others. She has the potential to be both a strong matriarch and a powerful presence in her own right. Her spiritual purpose will become more pronounced as she matures.

Judith can gain a great deal for herself by contributing to the care and protection of other people. Like Isis she is multi-faceted and can easily adapt to the changing roles and circumstances that she will face. The expression of her love and loyalty brings her much joy and facilitates her spiritual growth through her life.

6. SETH AND NEPHTHYS IN UNION

Khepri Reversed

This stone tablet indicates that many of Judith's greatest challenges come when she needs to motivate or stimulate the development of other people. This is an aspect of her work and personal roles that is understated and she may not always receive as much recognition or acknowledgement as she may like when she has contributed to the successes of others.

Although this is generally a positive placing, Khepri in this position may indicate some areas of frustration for Judith. She may attract other people who she considers to be unmotivated or whom she tries hard to motivate but with little obvious success. However, this is not always the case. She will learn a great deal about motivational skills, the nature of her own motives, drives and inspiration, and her ability to teach or manage other people. By motivating other people to heal themselves or improve their lives, Judith will bring healing improvements to herself and overcome any underlying resistance that she may have to her own personal development.

7. HORUS IN FLIGHT

Nephthys Upright

This stone indicates that Judith's ultimate spiritual direction is one of retreat and contemplation. The growth that comes to her through the activity that has been suggested by the other stone tablets in this reading is preparing Judith for a profound shift of consciousness. This change will come from assimilating her life's experiences and coming to terms with all her feelings.

The stone of Nephthys in this position indicates that Judith's soul is coming to a state of rest where she can find a new level of self-acceptance. By grieving for the losses and missed opportunities of the past, Judith can liberate herself from them and re-create herself in joy and blissful wonder.

Judith is creating a kind of spiritual stamina and an awareness of her own peace and stillness. Through contemplation, she will develop a new sense of harmony and trust that will help her to function in all of her relationships, whether business or personal, without jealousy or competition.

Nephthys guides Judith towards her highest potential and helps her to find greatest satisfaction by teaching her receptivity, stillness and humility. This placing strengthens Judith's ability to be compassionate and forgiving and stimulates her psychic, intuitive or healing abilities.

Overview

Judith's Eye of Horus spread indicates that she has chosen this lifetime as an opportunity to stimulate many changes in the world around her and, at the same time, come to a place of peace and stillness within herself. The stones chosen would suggest that she is quite an evolved soul, with a clear and balanced personality, who has chosen to face some powerful spiritual challenges in order to resolve unfinished business and move on to a higher plane of learning.

This spread indicates a lifetime of great service to others and a journey of powerful self-actualization. Judith may well become a champion of good causes and could easily assume a prominent public position. However, her ultimate peace, fulfilment and satisfaction is likely to come through periods of retreat from the world. She would be well advised to balance activity and service with stillness and contemplation.

Further Reading

EGYPTIAN MYTHOLOGY, CUSTOMS AND HIEROGLYPHIC SYMBOLS

The Ancient Egyptian Book of the Dead, R. O. Faulkner, British Museum Press, London, 1985 (Text originally published by The Limited Editions Club, New York, 1972).

A Dictionary of Egyptian Gods and Goddesses, George Hart, Routledge Kegan Paul Inc., London, 1986.

Discovering Egyptian Hieroglyphs, Karl-Theodor Zauzich, The University of Texas Press, 1992.

The Egyptian Book of the Dead, E. A. Wallis Budge, Dover Publications, New York, 1967 (from the translation originally published in 1895).

Egyptian Hieroglyphs: How to Read and Write Them, Stephane Rossini, Dover Publications, New York, 1989 (originally published by Editions Trimegiste, France, 1987).

Egyptian Myths (The Legendary Past), George Hart, British Museum Publications, London, 1990.

An Illustrated Dictionary of The Gods and Symbols of Ancient Egypt, Manfred Lurker, Thames and Hudson, London, 1980 (original German language edition published in 1974).

Practical Egyptian Magic, Murry Hope, Aquarian Press, Northamptonshire, England, 1984.

AFFIRMATIONS, VISUALIZATION AND THE USE OF POSITIVE THOUGHT TECHNIQUES

I See Myself in Perfect Health: Your Essential Guide to Self-healing, David Lawson, Thorsons, London, 1995.

Principles of Self-healing, David Lawson, Thorsons, London, 1996.

You Can Heal Your Life, Louise L. Hay, Hay House, California, 1984.

ASTROLOGY AND DIVINATION

Medicine Cards: The Discovery of Power Through the Ways of Animals, Jamie Sams and David Carson, Bear and Company, New Mexico, 1988.

Motherpeace: A Way to the Goddess through Myth, Art and Tarot, Vicki Noble, Harper Collins, New York, 1983.

Sacred Path Cards: The Discovery of Self Through Native Teachings, Jamie Sams, Harper Collins, New York, 1990.

Star Healing: Your Sun Sign, Your Health and Your Success, David Lawson, Hodder and Stoughton, London, 1994.

Tarot for Beginners, Kristyna Arcarti, Hodder and Stoughton, London, 1993.

The Tarot Reader, Nancy Shavick, Berkley, New York, 1991.

Sources

Page 9, chart: *Egyptian Gods and Myths*, Angela P. Thomas, Shire Publications, 1986; *The Penguin Guide to Ancient Egypt*, W. J. Murnane, Penguin Books, 1983.

Pages 11, 20 and 122, quotations: *The Ancient Egyptian Book of the Dead*, translated by R.O. Faulkner, British Museum Press, London, 1985; *The Egyptian Book of the Dead*, Translated by E. A. Wallis Budge, Dover Publications, Inc., 1967.

About the Author

David Lawson is an international healer and a teacher of personal development courses who has worked chiefly in the UK, Ireland, Spain and the USA. He is an authorized worldwide facilitator of Louise L. Hay's 'You Can Heal Your Life' study course programme. He is also a therapist, offering hands-on healing, counselling, meditational techniques and regression. David is the author of eight books including: *Star Healing – Your Sun Sign, Your Health and Your Success; Money and Your Life – A Prosperity Playbook* (with Justin Carson); *I See Myself in Perfect Health – Your Essential Guide to Self-healing; The Principles of Self-healing; The Principles of Your Psychic Potential* and *So You Want to be a Shaman*. His audio tapes include the guided visualizations *I See Myself in Perfect Health, Volumes I & II and the Money and Your Life Prosperity Course,* all published by Healing Workshops Press. For details of courses based upon *The Eye of Horus* and David's other self-healing and personal development material please write to Healing Workshops, PO Box 1678, London, NW5 4EW, UK.

'David Lawson takes you on a healing journey that everyone can benefit from.'
Louise L. Hay, author of *You Can Heal Your Life.*

Acknowledgements

I would like to thank the following people for their help
in the writing and publication of this book:
Susan Mears (my agent), Ian Jackson (my commissioning editor),
Sophie Bevan, Elaine Partington, Rachel Kirkland,
Pritty Ramjee, Aziz Khan, Sarah Howerd, Lilian and Eric Lawson,
Anne and Alex Carson, Doriane Beyer, Louise L. Hay
and all of my friends, family, clients and guides.
Special thanks to my partner Justin Carson whose practical support, ideas,
good humour and care make it possible for me to write.

EDDISON•SADD EDITIONS

Editorial Director Ian Jackson
Editor Sophie Bevan
Proofreader Michele Turney
Art Director Elaine Partington
Art Editor Pritilata Ramjee
Designer Rachel Kirkland
Illustrator Aziz Khan
Production Hazel Kirkman and Charles James

KEY TO THE STONE TABLETS

GEB
page 22

NUT
page 26

OSIRIS
page 30

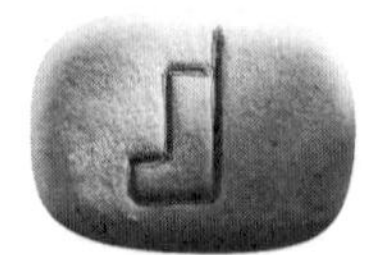
ISIS
page 34

SETH
page 38

NEPHTHYS
page 42

HORUS
page 46

BASTET
page 50

ANUBIS
page 54

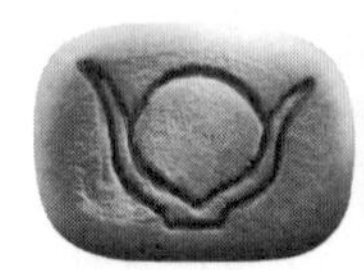
HATHOR
page 58

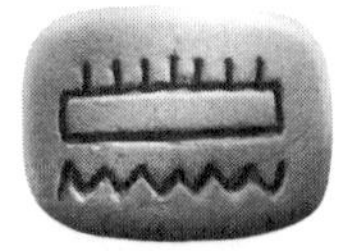
AMUN
page 62

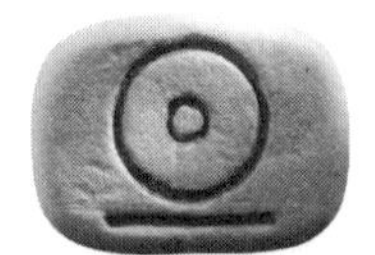
RE
page 66

KHONSU
page 70

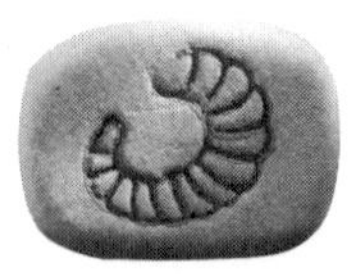
KHNUM
page 74

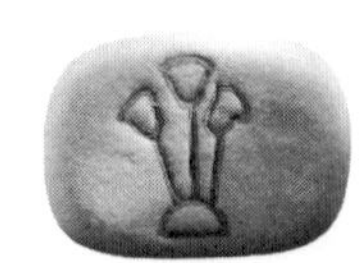
HAPY
page 78

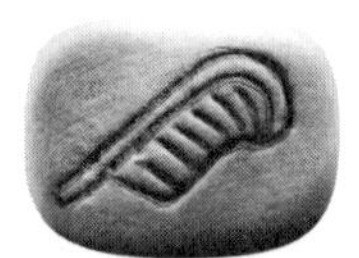
MAAT
page 82

KHEPRI
page 86

ANAT
page 90

MIN
page 94

HEKET
page 98

APIS
page 102

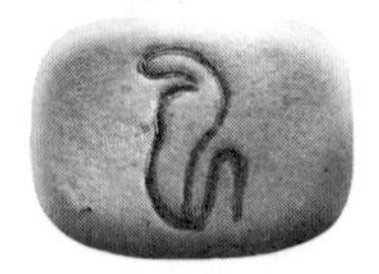
MERETSEGER
page 106

IMHOTEP
page 110

THE PYRAMIDS
page 114

THE SPHINX
page 118